Best Wishes
Steve Cui

HEINEMANN

SCHOOL

MANAGEMENT

Primary School Management

MIKE HARRISON
AND STEVE GILL

Heinemann Educational Books Ltd
Halley Court, Jordan Hill, Oxford OX2 8EJ

OXFORD LONDON EDINBURGH
MADRID ATHENS BOLOGNA PARIS
MELBOURNE SYDNEY AUCKLAND
IBADAN NAIROBI HARARE GABORONE
SINGAPORE TOKYO PORTSMOUTH NH (USA)

94 95 96 11 10 9 8 7 6 5 4 3

A catalogue record for this book is available from the British Library

ISBN 0-435-80960-1
Produced by **AMR Ltd**
Printed in England by Clays Ltd., St Ives plc

Contents

1 Planning for school development

In recent years, the role of the primary Headteacher has changed rapidly and radically. *The Education Reform Act 1988* and the *Education No 2 Act 1986* broadened the responsibilities of the Head substantially. The Head who once saw herself first and foremost as an excellent teacher, influencing the work of other teachers, is now a budget holder and school manager, expected to build, lead, inspire and motivate a teaching team; balance priorities for time, money and human resources; manage the school building and equipment; promote the school to the local community; plan the curriculum and supervise its delivery, record keeping and assessment; and to make sure that all of this provides excellent education for her children. The demands are challenging and could be overwhelming.

This book is based on our experience in managing primary schools and on the inservice training we have provided for current and would-be managers. It is designed to equip the reader with ideas, suggestions and structures for coping with the demands placed upon them, and to help them in turn, provide the children in their care with a happy and worthwhile experience of school in their primary years.

We begin by stepping back to look at the school as a whole, and its development plan.

The planning cycle

The most realistic of timescales for making definite plans for development, is three years. Longer than this, and unforeseeable changes in personnel and priorities, can make plans prematurely irrelevant.

Effective planning involves two discrete processes:

1   **Initial planning** – based on review and development principles providing a benchmark or baseline for change.

2   **The maintenance process** – continuous evaluation and

development which drives the process forward, sustaining the best practice and seeking to improve the less effective.

▉ The development plan structure

This recommended framework is based on the original guidelines from the DES, modified in the light of experience. It also takes into account the recommendations of the School Development Plans Project in a paper called *The Management and Development of Planning*, published by the Department of Education and Science in April 1990.

The plan consists of four main sections each including a range of elements:

A   Curriculum
Audit of current practice
Identification of required changes
Revision of schemes of work as necessary
Place of cross-curricular themes
Priorities for change
Timetable for change

B   Organisation
Grouping of pupils for teaching and learning
Special Educational Needs provision and arrangements
Thematic and subject specific teaching
Time allocation for teaching
Subject balance

C   Assessment and record keeping
School policy on assessment and recording pupil progress
Moderating between teachers
Internal transfer of information between teachers
Links between feeder/receiving schools
Portfolios of evidence
Records of Achievement/Pupil Profiling
Reporting to parents

D   Management
Material resources
Identification of needs
Priorities for change and identified timescale
Provisions of job descriptions for teaching staff
Examination of roles/job description for:

- ancillary staff
- support teachers
- secretary
- caretaker

Identification of shortage areas: specialist skills

Appraisal and staff development - INSET implications

▓ The whole school review

This rather daunting process is more manageable if it is broken down into specific questions and tasks. We suggest the systematic analysis that follows. It can be followed closely or used as a prompt or *aide-memoire*. It is particularly effective if all the staff are involved in the review, either individually or in small groups. The key to staff commitment, in this as in all matters, is staff involvement. Where better to start than with the baseline review of the school in which they work.

▶ **Every school of course has always had 'aims', even if they are often not formally stated. Now they must be so worded and resolved by the governors. The Education Act of 1986 requires in Section 18 that the Governors consider the aims of the school, and this legal requirement to draft specific aims is a helpful practical step in reviewing the school and planning for the future.**

A   Curriculum

- State in outline form, **current curriculum provision** for CORE and FOUNDATION subjects, plus Religious Education.

- Prepare reactions to the LEA's Curriculum Policy for the Governors.

- Consider each subject in turn, and assess the extent to which what is currently taught matches the **National Curriculum Programmes of Study**.

- Where gaps exist between current practice and statutory requirements, plan a programme of revision or preparation of **schemes of work** (see Chapter 10).

- Assess the effectiveness of **cross-curricular themes** and the teaching of non-foundation subjects, for example, in Personal and Social Education.

- Indicate a **timetable** for the implementation of any required changes, stating priorities where necessary.

B   Organisation

- Consider the **grouping of pupils** for teaching and learning. Is the current class structure the most effective? If you have vertical grouping, is it for educational reasons or purely organisational necessity? Does your system allow for flexible alternatives on occasions – team teaching, specialist teaching? Setting? (See Chapter 8.)

- What arrangements are there for children identified as having **Special Educational Needs**? Are children with statements adequately catered for? Are children without statements having their needs met? What provision do you make for the most able? Identify necessary changes.

- Identify subjects taught through an integrated or *thematic approach*. What proportion of the curriculum is delivered in this way? Is there a common policy throughout the school? Do groups/teams of teachers plan cooperatively? Which subjects are taught separately? Is the appropriate proportion of teaching time devoted to thematic as opposed to a subject specific approach (See Chapter 10). Identify necessary changes.

- Consider the times of sessions of the school day. Does the total of *teaching time* match legal requirements? Analyze the distribution of teaching time within the pupil day. Is it being planned to the best effect? Is afternoon break really necessary? How can teacher non-contact time be created and used to maximum effect?

- Consider individual pupil timetables at different stages (age groups) and provide a statement of *subject balance*. This could be a percentage analysis. Are your findings satisfactory? Identify ncessary changes.

C   Assessment and record keeping

- Does the school have a **policy** for record keeping and assessment in place? Has an assessment coordinator been appointed? Do recording schedules meet the needs of teachers? For which subjects do they apply? Do they need revising or simplifying in the light of experience? Has the LEA issued guidelines, and if so, has maximum benefit been gained from them?

- Examine **moderation** between teachers with respect to assessment. This is particularly necessary where parallel classes exist. Do teachers plan together for assessment? Do they compare their pupils' work? Is this a predetermined part of the work of the school or an ad hoc arrangement? One staff meeting per half term for moderation is a most valuable use of time.

- Formal records form a crucial part of the information passed **between teachers**. Are they easily understood? Do all use the same systems? (See policy.) Is some material superfluous and kept for the sake of it? Would pupils' interest be better served if some material was pruned? What is the basic minimum record that is necessary to serve the pupils' best interests (See Chapter 8).

- Links between **feeder and receiving schools** are important, but too much information can lead to vital bits being overlooked. Will your records be understood by others? Are they informative yet succinct? If examples of pupils' work are passed on, will they be appreciated or consigned to the bin? (See Records of Achievement/portfolios of evidence below.) Identify necessary changes.

- **Portfolios** of evidence are required to substantiate teacher assessment of National Curriculum Attainment Target levels. Is the quantity of work collected manageable? How is it stored? Some schools have become over-zealous, even obsessed, with the need to record and retain everything - audio/photographic even video records where written evidence is not available. Do I trust sufficiently in the professionalism of my staff to resist such a temptation?

- Schools will have considered introducing a system of pupil profiling or **Records of Achievement**. Does our system celebrate achievement? Are pupils involved in making judgements about their own work? Do parents have a role to play and do they participate regularly? What mechanisms have been created to give parents a real insight into their children's education?

- You are required by law to report annually to parents. Have you devised your own summative **reporting document** or are you using the DES/LEA offering? Does it provide sufficient room for teacher comment? Does the pupil have a say? At what stage does the parent make a comment? Does the Headteacher's summary follow the teacher's final comment or the parents' reply? What happens to the report at the end of the process?

D   Management

- Your development plan will need to make an assessment of the **material resources** available and required to implement the curriculum. Local management provides more flexibility to make resourcing decisions (See Chapter 9). Do you have a policy for resource allocation? Do curriculum coordinators have a role to play? Have you decided upon a timescale for furniture replacement and decorating programmes? Do you have enough computers to support the curriculum through IT? Your audit of resources must consider all aspects including accommodation, books, materials, equipment, IT and home economics' facilities, libraries, etc.

- Your most important resource is human. Do all your teaching staff have **job descriptions**? Are outline job descriptions available to all members of staff, so everyone is aware of the responsibilities of others? How often are detailed job descriptions renegotiated? (See Chapter 2.)

- It is equally important to issue job descriptions to **non-teaching staff**. Are ancillary staff (NNEBs etc.) clear about their roles and responsibilities? Have you reviewed the role of any support teachers attached to the school recently? Are job descriptions available for the school secretary and caretaker? It will be particularly important to consider the role of the secretary who has been put under tremendously increased pressure by recent changes. Can she cope? What support can you offer? Does the budget allow for extra hours, an additional clerical assistant – perhaps part-time? Should your secretary be regraded in recognition of her additional responsibilities?

- Identify shortage areas of specialised skills. Do you have a policy for systematic analysis of **specialist skill** requirements, when making new appointments? Can you use your knowledge of team role theory (See Chapter 3) to build a better team spirit? Is there a balance of specialisms across Key Stages 1 and 2? Can coordinators work in pairs rather than individually to give more effective curriculum cover? A useful strategy here is to establish a principal and an assistant coordinator for each subject, where one teacher is responsible for KS1 and the other for KS2. Not only do they provide a wider spread of experience and have more credibility with the staff, but they are able to offer one another support and encouragement. In all but the very large schools, such a policy would mean each member of staff having two coordinator roles – e.g. principal coordinator for maths and assistant coordinator for geography.

- Performance appraisal is a legal requirement (See Chapter 6.) **Staff development** needs are an integral part of school development. How do you identify INSET priorities? Are you able to differentiate between institutional needs and individual needs? Whilst recognising that the principal focus of INSET is the school, can you satisfy individual teacher's particular requirement for personal development? A system which frustrates individual team members in their desire for personal development is heading for trouble.

▉ Development or maintenance?

Having undertaken an analysis of whole-school review the next question is: How much change is required, and how soon?

Headteachers must be cautious of being stampeded into too much change, too quickly. People can only cope with a relatively small number of innovations simultaneously. Too much too soon leads to 'innovation overload syndrome'. The symptoms of this syndrome are all too easy to detect, with a marked decline in staff morale being the primary indicator.

The most effective schools are those in which there exists a natural equilibrium between development and maintenance. These schools will be more likely to respond favourably and successfully to development planning. If a school becomes too obsessed with development, it is likely to become unstable because of its neglect of continuity. Conversely a school which wishes only to preserve the status quo will be unable to respond to genuine imperatives for change.

The Schools Development Plans paper *The Management of Devlopment Planning*, published by the DES, offers detailed guidance on how a successful school will achieve this balance in eight key areas of its activities:

1 Aims

The fact that schools have multiple and diffuse aims is a strength of the system. However, strategies have to be developed to achieve them over a period of time with one or more aims being considered in detail as part of a phased programme.

2 The role of partners

There will always be tension between the expectations of the various client groups (Government, DES, LEA, Governors, Parents, Pupils and Local Community). The school recognises these different expectations and strives to achieve a balance between responding to them and explaining the school's position.

3 Curriculum

The school aims to devlop whole-school policies which will bring the staff together. This is particularly important when external pressure for curriculum change is strong. Effective schools adopt a whole-school response and strategies are developed which are supported by everyone.

4 Organisation

Changes in organisation come about in response to clearly perceived needs rather than whim or fancy. Changes which evolve slowly, following a pilot which has been successfully evaluated, are likely to achieve most support and stand the greatest chance of being accepted by the majority.

5 School management

Clear lines of responsibility exist but all members of staff feel valued. A spirit of colleageality exists alongside this structure of responsibility and accountability. The management of the school is shared, with leadership being delegated as circumstances dictate, without the Headteacher abdicating responsibility for the school as a whole.

6 Innovation and change

The school builds innovation onto existing good practice after collective deliberation. Successful change is that which survives the departure of the original innovators. The school does not engage in so many innovations that it is overwhelmed by them. Change should only proceed at a rate which will enable evaluation to take place.

7 Support systems

The staff development policy supports a limited range of innovation to meet the school's needs. School-basd INSET is emphasised rather than too many teachers attending external courses to enhance their own professional development. The number of occasions when classes are taught by supply teachers whilst staff are out of school is kept strictly under review.

8 Ethos

A product of shared values and commitments of the school and its partners. Ethos is a two-way process. It both supports appropriate development and change and is improved by the activity.

■ Conclusion

Schools will always need to respond to continually changing circumstances. Planning for school development is therefore the most important aspect of the role of the Headteacher. To manage this development effectively, Headteachers need to acquire a range of skills and strategies. Schools are complex organisations but the management task is achievable.

This book breaks down the daunting management challenge into its constituent parts and offers skills, methods, structures and roles for measurable success in improving and managing your school as a combined teaching unit.

2 Appointing staff

It has often been said that a Headteacher's reputation is made or lost by his ability to recruit, retain and motivate staff. Imagine that you are the Head of Belle Vista Primary and the time has come for you to show your mettle. Miss Cluttock has announced her intention to retire at the end of next term. The making of a new appointment has to become your first priority and needs to absorb much of your attention over the next few months. You must work out the most effective strategy to achieve your aims for the school.

To start with you will need to review the roles played by your existing staff and take stock of how far the school has developed under your leadership. What needs to be done next? What will the staff profile look like without Miss Cluttock? Notwithstanding recent legislation, you will make a crucial mistake if you believe that it is up to anyone else to arrange for the vacancy to be filled and to make the most effective appointment. Your Deputy may have a job description which includes *'to assist in the appointment of staff'*, you may have a most competent and interested governing body or may even be blessed with highly prescriptive selection procedure laid down by your LEA. Despite any of these, the responsibility to select the right person and to set up a procedure so to do, lies with one person. YOU.

■ Prepare the ground

An excellent starting point is to begin with the person who is leaving. With a departing member of staff you have a new resource. You may elicit from her the strengths and weaknesses of various aspects of the school (now she knows she will not have to put them right) and understand further the contribution to the school this teacher has made, or thinks she has made. If any remedial action is called for, try to take it before her replacement starts. You will, of course, be able to offer your personal congratulations and thank her for her work in the school.

This may go some way to secure the teacher's goodwill for future supply work and enhance your caring image amongst the staff. Les Bell gives an excellent description of the rationale of an exit interview and a schedule for its execution in his book *Management Skills in Primary Schools*.

APPOINTMENT CHECKLIST

	Accept resignation, arrange and carry out **exit interview**.
WEEK 1	Discuss vacancy with Senior Management Team. Make out draft list of requirements for post. Contact Chair of Governors to discuss results of meeting and place advert in liaison with LEA. Draw up further particulars and job description. Make arrangements to note names of enquirers and to send out application forms and particulars. Draw up person specification in conjunction with LEA, SMT and governing body.
WEEK 3	Review applications to create **long list** and send for confidential reports from referees.
WEEK 5	Convene meeting to draw up **short list** of suitable candidates for interview. Liaise with LEA and Chair of Governors to find suitable date for interviews. Invite shortlisted candidates to attend. Set up procedures for applicants to visit the school.
WEEK 8	Hold interviews.

Consider the strategy

A vacancy is a real opportunity to bring about a level of change which can be difficult in other circumstances. One aspect which you must now consider, is whether to make any appointment at all. Your tightly pressed governing body may view this vacancy as a godsend to make a saving on the expenditure account. Teachers are the school's most expensive resource. Can you afford to fill the post? Will finance be available in subsequent years? How expensive in personal and financial costs will it be to make a new teacher redundant if the number of children on roll decreases substantially? Can Miss Cluttock's job be worked around in the short term or long term? Is a permanent appointment needed or would it be better to advertise for a temporary post for the time being? Will this affect the number and quality of applicants you may attract?

Such decisions will colour the next phase in the appointment process – getting the right candidates to apply. Selecting and appointing staff brings together the two essential aspects of organisational life – namely people and purpose. The exit interview with Miss Cluttock was illuminating, particularly her views on the curriculum area which, up until now, you had understood to be her responsibility. Her admission that she copied the curriculum document from her friend's school instead of 'having all these meetings' was most illuminating, especially when she added – just like everyone else does!

▉ Consult the staff

Now is the time to consult with your Senior Management Team (SMT) as to how the opportunities created by this vacancy can be utilised to maximum effect.

There may be general agreement amongst the senior staff, that the most useful way to approach the new situation would be to have a teacher without class responsibility. This would necessitate slightly larger classes, but afford continuity of supply cover in case of absence (resulting in a saving), provide time for coordinators to become more involved in each other's classes for curriculum leadership and give some individual support for children with Special Needs.

If this is seen as a positive option, then it will probably need to be sold to the remaining staff. Teachers always believe their classes are too big; some forceful and convincing arguments may need to be employed. The SMT may wish to conduct a survey amongst staff to determine their view of the strengths and weaknesses of the school, and to ascertain their priorities. This may well ease in any newcomer and ensure a unanimity of purpose. The incoming teacher will better adjust to the role if all his or her new colleagues have similar expectations of the part he or she will play. As Headteacher you will also be better placed when facing the governing body, if you are able to demonstrate that all the staff are behind the proposed plan.

Alternatively, circumstances may dictate the necessity to appoint a teacher to assume responsibility for Miss Cluttock's class. This will almost certainly be the case if the vacancy arises mid-year.

Consideration also needs to be given to the question of whether an incentive allowance should be offered, if indeed one is available. This issue is one of the most delicate matters you may have to handle. In almost every case when an incentive allowance becomes available, you will be faced with the conflict between promoting an existing member of staff (a negotiation strategy) or using it as bait (a recruitment device).

Generalised advice is of little value. Precedent may be set in one case, such that teachers may come to expect that they will end up with allowances by 'Buggin's Turn'. In another case staff may see themselves as undervalued and feel that the only way to get promotion is to leave. Each decision will be unique. Too much care cannot be exercised in this matter, as an ill-judged appointment to a promoted post can generate shock waves within your existing staff team, which can reverberate for a considerable time.

Consult the governing body

Now that you have some definite ideas it is time to approach Major Dunwody, your Chair of Governors.

You may begin by reporting the steps you have taken so far and your immediate thoughts. As well as being able to justify the role you want the appointee to play, you may well have to demonstrate that the school will stay within budget. It may be appropriate at this point to discuss and agree with him the detail of the simple advertisement to be placed in the educational press.

Place the advertisement

Your LEA will probably have a policy with regard to advertising posts, and will be able to offer advice. If you are making your first appointment, you may be surprised at just how long the process will take from the placing of that initial advert until you choose the person you want. Eight weeks is by no means unusual. This is not because people are dilatory but because various stages have to be gone through before other processes can start. (See checklist.)

Write the job description

Whilst waiting for your advertisement to be printed and for teachers to respond, you should prepare the job specification which will form part of the mailing which will be sent to those interested. From the experience she gained as a Senior Inspector, Joan Dean emphasises, in her book *Managing the Primary School*, that this should be composed with care. In cases where teachers are not performing satisfactorily and disciplinary procedures are instituted, she reminds us that the job description is a major piece of evidence.

It is essential that a job description should be written in such a way that it remains capable of later negotiation. In the first instance, however, this format will be appropriate:

> Title of post:
> Salary (+ incentive allowance):
> Person to whom the post holder will be responsible:
> Purpose of the post:
> Responsibilities for:
>   teaching role
>   curriculum area
>   other activities
>   work of other teachers
>   equipment, materials, etc.

This outline description can now be tested on your senior colleagues and a copy mailed to the Chair of Governors.

The purpose of the initial advert is to inform teachers who wish to advance their careers or would like to move to your area, that there is a vacancy at your school. The secondary mailing is designed to attract properly qualified and experienced people who have an interest in the particular fields you have specified. You will want to stress the attractiveness of the post, the school and the local area, but without making any promises that the job cannot deliver. The details you give will serve to discourage potentially unsuitable candidates.

Think carefully about the information you supply. The following checklist will help:

- Some information about the Local Authority;
- Name and address of school;
- Type of school, group size, numbers on roll over the past few years, staffing establishment, the school and its situation;
- History of school, any significant events;

- Description of site and buildings – age, features, split site, future plans, school catchment area;
- Age range of school, numbers in each year, method of organisation – horizontal/vertical grouping;
- Feeder arrangements with nursery, infant, junior, secondary schools;
- Community/church involvement including use of premises;
- Achievements and initiatives of which the school is proud.

Staffing

- Establishment and number of permanent staff in post;
- Structure of management team and incentive allowances – where this post fits into this scheme.

Home - school liaison

- PTA, parents' education meetings, parents' evenings;
- Expectation of teacher involvement.

Curriculum

- Brief statement about aspects of the school's curriculum relevant to the post.

This checklist is adapted from one of those recommended in the POST report published in 1983.

In addition you may wish to give candidates some advice about how to complete their application form. You will be familiar with forms from your own LEA but not all candidates will be. Are there specific things you would like to see in the candidate's letter of application? Would you like to elicit their ideas about the role of a coordinator for early years, home - school links or assessment? Is it important that they expand upon any responsibility they have had for the work of others? Ask about this now.

▉ Prepare for the visits

You will need to prepare for visits to the school by potential applicants. In any case shortlisted candidates should be invited to visit the school, preferably during the working day. Tell your staff when this will happen. Some teachers are extremely touchy about this, and unfortunately not always as courteous in their dealings with visitors as you might like. Talk to them about the promotion of Belle Vista's image and the importance to you all of attracting the right person. Chris Day et al stress in *Managing Primary Schools* that *'a teaching vacancy is a staffing problem only those willing to leave their present employment can solve.'* It may be opportune to remind all those involved of this point. Perhaps schools are not always as grateful as they might be to those volunteering to put themselves out to solve **their** staffing problem.

Decide who is the most suitable person to show the candidate around the school. One successful approach is to release a teacher of the same grade as the post advertised (but not Mrs Fischer, who will have the post pro-tem and has also applied). This teacher can tell the applicant what it is really like to work with you and give a teacher's perspective on the school. The arrangements for each visit will, of course, vary with the time of day but should include the following:

- A tour of the building and grounds;
- An opportunity to see staff and children at work;
- A chance to talk with the children the successful candidate would be teaching;
- A meeting with the departing teacher;
- A chat with the staff at play or lunchtime;
- A talk with the Headteacher.

Such a tour will feed the conversation you will have with the candidate. You will then be able to use the visit to make some initial judgements. This is, of course, an informal pre-interview but one which cuts both ways. Both the Headteacher and candidate are in a much better position by the end of the visit to assess the situation. A traditional twenty-minute interview leaves a lot of room for misunderstanding and false impressions and any additional evidence which can be gained from spending this time (in a more natural environment) will be most valuable.

■ Agree the criteria for selection

The short-listing process at Belle Vista Primary may be either a simple or complex process depending on the size of the selection panel and the number and quality of applications. As with most issues you will find it a lot easier if you have a clear understanding of what you are after. The person specification comes into its own at this point. Get it agreed by the panel beforehand, then start short-listing by ruthlessly sticking to the criteria you have set. The school may be enhanced by recruiting someone with a black belt in origami but not at the expense of getting an experienced reception teacher with an expertise in science, which is what you wanted.

Many people make the mistake of sorting through the pile of applications to choose the best four or six. As Headteacher you should resist this at all costs. If only three people are suitable for the post, then you will not want to invite lay governors to interview and perhaps appoint one of the others. Try to arrange criteria-referenced selection according to your person profile so that this cannot occur. If you are lucky enough to have a surplus of suitable candidates, it is then the time to discuss how many people you can afford to interview to be sure of choosing the best.

▓ Assess the applications against the criteria

Age/sex

These may be the first characteristics of the application your governors notice. It may be necessary for you to make explicit to them that these factors are not significant.

Experience

Has the candidate taught the age range you specify, is his/her experience of other ages of children transferable, is his/her experience in depth or width? Has the candidate taught in more than one school? Can any inferences be drawn from this?

Qualifications

Has the candidate engaged in further studies since leaving initial training? What does this imply? Is there any use of which this further study has been put in his/her present school?

Achievements/responsibilities

What had the candidate achieved in his/her current position? Has he/she been responsible for the work of others? How was this done?

Potential

Are these aspects of this application which impress you as to the future worth of this candidate?

In addition, there may be other factors which you decide to consider. These may include a candidate's outside interests, church connections, professional and personal development record or extra-curricular activities.

A summary sheet will aid objectivity when comparing candidates, especially when the task is being undertaken by more than one person.

NAME			
QUALIFICATIONS			
TEACHING EXPERIENCE			
RESPONSIBILITIES / ACHIEVEMENTS			
CURRICULAR SPECIALISMS			
INTERESTS OUTSIDE EDUCATION			
EXTRA-CURRICULAR ACTIVITIES			
EVIDENCE OF POTENTIAL / EXTRAS			

■ Agree the panel

The type of interview conducted will depend on many factors. You may find that appointment procedures are tightly prescribed by rules of governance or LEA regulations, or you may have sufficient flexibility to determine procedures for yourself.

Some governors are unable to make daytime meetings, other newly-appointed governors may not wish to be involved. It may be possible to get governing bodies to set up an appointment subcommittee for most posts, consisting of the Headteacher, Chair and one other member.

You need to consider the position of teacher-governors here. Democratically, teacher-governors need to be treated in just the same way as any other governor. We cannot have two classes of governors: those entitled to take part in the selection process and those not. In particular, teacher-governors will have an idea as to the sort of person who would fit into the existing staff team. Yet there are professional niceties. If the appointment is for say, the Deputy Head, should a teacher hear critical voices raised about the qualities of her future line manager? Will teacher-governors be put in an invidious position by reading confidential reports on their superiors or teachers currently on their own staff? The law does intervene to some degree. If the post is one in which an appointment might be to the advantage of the teacher-governor herself, then she is automatically excluded.

Let's consider an example. Miss Cluttock held a 'B' allowance as Head of Infants. Pauline Smith, already on the staff, is to be interviewed for the post. If she is appointed, then her 'A' allowance becomes available and Mrs Dunwin (the teacher-governor) may feel she is in a good position to be awarded such an allowance. Thus there is clearly some self interest here and the teacher-governor should not be allowed to be part of the interview panel. The position of a more senior teacher (say Mr Jolly 'B' allowance) is less clear. It could be argued that there is no reason to exclude him as he would not gain from an internal appointment. However, with the increased flexibility provided under LMS, the vacated 'A' allowance money could be added to his 'B' to create a 'C' allowance which previously the school could not afford. Mr Jolly could well have an interest in this case. Good sense needs to prevail. It is not unknown for panels to decide to avoid the issue by holding interviews during the school day when teacher-governors are in class, or in August when they are on holiday!

■■ Prepare for the interview

Having constructed a short-list, arrangements for the interviews will have to be made. It is easy to overlook important matters in the excitement of your first appointment and therefore the following checklist is provided as an *aide memoire*:

Essential points are in ordinary script, options are in italics:

Interview checklist

- Consult with the LEA representative and Chair of Governors to fix date.

- Write to referees to ask for confidential reports on the candidates. Tell them the date of the interviews *and include a job description, profile of the school and any particular points about which you would like them to comment.*

- Write to candidates telling them date, time and place *and to whom to report on arrival. If you want them to bring anything with them, such as diplomas or examples of children's work, say so here.*

- *Inform candidates of names of interviewers and other interviewees, invite them to look around the school if they have not been already, send school brochure, curriculum document as appropriate to post, include transport directions to the school and expense claim form.*

- *Prepare pack(s) to be sent to reserve candidates if short-listed applicants are unable to atten*d.

- Write to members of the selection panel *including those with whom you fixed the date.* Include date, time *(tell them half hour before first interview)*, name/number of room that interviews will be held in and to where members should go on arrival. *Include in the mailing the job description and person specifications, a list of the candidates, interview schedule, copy of all items sent to interviewees, photocopies of application forms, minutes of any meeting held to discuss appointment to be made, along with instructions to bring each of these items to the interview.*

- Arrange for someone - teacher, secretary, caretaker, PTA secretary to be in attendance to service candidates and panel.

- Make arrangements for a suitably furnished room to be available with some protection from disturbance, and refreshments to be on hand.

- Meet with the panel beforehand. Establish with the Chair the format of the interview. Who is to see candidates in and out, arrange introductions? Establish the pattern of questioning, ensure that each interview will be conducted on similar lines and end appropriately. Make sure the panel are clear about your needs for the post before the first candidate is interviewed.

- *Meet with inexperienced Chair of Governors to ensure that protocol and procedure are understood. Ensure that she/he understands that questions of a political/religious/sexual/union nature are not permissible.*

- *Meet with inexperienced panel members beforehand and discuss nature of appointment and any current educational jargon which may be used.*

- *Meet with interviewees beforehand to remind them that they will be dealing with lay people and that they should explain their answers clearly.* Ensure that the overall interview structure is understood by everyone. One person needs to be charged with summing up at the end. Voting procedures need to be in place in case a unanimous decision cannot be reached.

■ Interview the candidates

This book cannot provide suitable questions to ask at interview. Too much depends on the individual requirements of the post to be filled. There are, however, some guiding principles which you should be aware of. You have done the hard work in short-listing a group of people who you think can do the job. The task of interviewing is to allow them to give of their best and to impress the panel. To do this it will be necessary to try to relax the candidates. The Chair should be asked to do this as each candidate begins his/her interview.

Try to ensure that each member of the panel, such as parents, LEA governors, foundation church governors, adviser, etc. is encouraged to ask questions representing their sectional interest. In this way a balance of questions should emerge.

Remind panel members that the object of the exercise is to allow the candidates to do most of the talking. Questions should be short and lead to open-ended answers.

Questions can be ones that check on factual information; allow for opinion; explore candidates' attitudes; encourage argument and give an opportunity for interviewees to show what they can do under pressure.

The panel must be made aware of NO GO areas before the first interview. (It is too late for at least one candidate if you wait until an incident arises.)

Questions to avoid include:

- Which union do you belong to?
- At 35 most men are married....?
- What will you do if your children become ill?
- Have you ever gone on strike?
- Are you a Christian?
- What does your husband think of you going for promotion?
- Do you belong to a political party?
- What do you think of the government's effort to improve education?
- How can you teach these types of children to be British?

■ Making your choice

The criteria for short-listing will of course apply when making your choice at interview. In addition you will have the benefit of references, the information you gained from the informal visit and the candidate's performance at interview. His or her energy, vitality, ease with people, performance under pressure, confidence and consistency may be revealed during the interview. Your choice may not be the initial choice of all the panel, but whatever the final decision turns out to be, you should encourage the Chair to make sure that the decision is properly agreed on and that the successful candidate feels that he or she has the support of all of you in the selection.

■ After the interview

One of the panel has to take responsibility for thanking the unsuccessful candidates and if possible giving them feedback on their performance.

In the meantime you will want to spend some time with the appointee, not least to congratulate them and start to build up a relationship. You will need to check that you have all the information you need to get the appointee onto the payroll from the appropriate time and set up some dates when the new teacher can meet the staff, be introduced to the children and gain access to the premises before starting.

Finally do not omit to write to unsuccessful applicants not interviewed thanking them for their interest, wishing them well in future applications and telling them the name of the successful appointee.

■ Induction

When a new member of staff arrives many things change. Existing staff nearly always take a step upwards on the informal seniority ladder. By the way in which they know the ropes and transmit that information to newer members of staff they can increase their personal influence. This may be exactly what you want to happen, but it is also important that new members of staff are given a systematic introduction into the ways of the school.

■ Background reading for newly appointed staff

Presenting documents to newly-appointed staff has to be managed effectively. Information needs to be phased so that the load is manageable.

Our experience suggests that documents are given to the newly-appointed teacher at three different times.

On appointment/on first visit

School Policy Documents, e.g.

curriculum areas
admissions
behaviour
assemblies, uniform, school trips, etc.
School Development Plan
School brochure for parents
Staff members and their responsibilities
Names of non-teaching staff and roles
National Curriculum Development Plan
Records of children in class to be taught
Management structure of school
Holiday dates list

On taking up post

Minutes of last staff meeting(s)
National Curriculum subject files
National Curriculum Assessment folder
Records of Achievement Guidelines
Method of ordering both consumable and capital items
List of computer programs available
TV, hall, playground-duty timetables

Second term in post / before only if needed

LEA guidance documents, e.g.
equal opportunities
special needs
curriculum entitlement, etc.
INSET policy – method of applying
INSET opportunities – courses available
School traditions – Christmas, last day of term, elderly persons'
concert, etc.
Minutes of Governors' meetings
PTA meetings and functions

Your school and situation may demand a different system of phasing, or you may wish to leave this decision to a mentor.

Appointing a mentor

The concept of mentoring is new and could offer some real

advantages. The idea is to choose another member of staff who will protect, advise and guide the newly-appointed teacher. You may wish to appoint a different person each time the need arises or to tie this role to a permanent incentive allowance, including extending the role to all new staff, probationary teachers and students. You will want to choose a mentor who exhibits qualities which you hope your newly-appointed teacher will emulate. Loyalty to you or to the school, willingness to explore new ideas, good work habits, good classroom practice and a positive example of staff leadership may all be traits you look for in selecting a mentor.

In choosing one member of staff against another you will be signalling a strong preference, so choose your mentor with care. The most important quality, however, must be an ability to relate to people. To induct the new teacher successfully into the school culture, the quality of the interpersonal skills of the mentor will be the key to success. The ability to counsel adults in a professional atmosphere may take a while to develop and mistakes will occur along the way. Such a person will need to be rewarded for taking on this role. Financial rewards may not be possible or appropriate. Some teachers may be persuaded that experience in this field will help them to present themselves as potential candidates as lecturers or advisory teachers. Others might be convinced that they will benefit from this addition to their experience to gain promotion within the school system. However, the most persuasive inducement you can offer is to give your mentor the time to do the job properly. It may involve working alongside staff in the classroom, especially students and probationary teachers. It will involve time in helping the new teacher to become acclimatised to the peculiarities of Belle Vista. Expecting this to be done at weekends, evening, breaks and in chance meetings in the corridor is unrealistic and also downgrades the value you place on this role. It is in your interests to make the appointment as effective as possible, as soon as possible. Time spent in this way, choosing the right person to act as mentor and releasing her for guaranteed periods from her class-teaching duties will be well rewarded.

■ Conclusion

In this chapter we have led you through the process of identifying the opportunities provided by a retiring member of staff, filling the vacancy and inducting the new member of staff. Now you need to consider the way in which you can build the staff into a team. This is the subject of the next chapter.

3 Building and leading a professional team

Before reading this chapter:

TASK ONE

Ask your probationer, or least experienced teacher, to brainstorm a list of favoured characteristics which ought to be found in the Headteacher of an effective school, seal the list in an envelope, and give the envelope to you.

TASK TWO

Brainstorm your own list of ideal qualities and characteristics which you think a 'SuperHead' should possess. Ideas which you can endorse and aspire to. Now grit your teeth and underline those areas in which you feel the need for personal development. Put your list in a safe place.

■■ Leadership styles

Whether you are an established manager, newly appointed, or someone contemplating the greasy pole of promotion, you are certain to have one thing in common. A genuine desire to lead. Motives are complex and varied, and range from a vague sense of having something to offer the community, to a burning certainty that you have the answer to the malaise which is currently choking the system! In any event you need to decide on your own particular Leadership Style.

Of course 'deciding' is a rather too simplistic notion. We all have a natural style with which we feel most at home. Left to their own devices people tend to fall into one of the three classic categories first identified in 1944 by Lewin. There have been a number of refinements of this basic theory since then, but the original descriptions are satisfactory for our purposes.

They are:

> **AUTOCRATIC**
> **LAISSEZ-FAIRE**
> **DEMOCRATIC**

Let us examine how they can be applied to the management of primary schools.

Those of us who have been teaching for a few years will have come across most of these characters.

■ Deidre the Despot

Remember the old autocrat you used to work for? (Yes, work *for*, none of this modern egalitarian nonsense about working *with*). Feared. Respected. Held in awe. It is sometimes tempting to look back through rose tints and recall those glorious summer days of yesteryear. Easy to forget having to queue up on Monday morning for stock, and being required to send the children to the Head's office with their worn-down pencil stubs before they could have a replacement.

More importantly, were you involved in any decision making? Did you feel involved? Were your views either sought or valued?

Probably not.

■ Anything goes Jo

I doubt if you recall this character so fondly. Spent most of her time wandering around aimlessly, 'making allowances' for children because of their deprived social background. Liked laying on treats even when undeserved. Always had an expression of injured incomprehension when the staffroom was still fully occupied ten minutes after the end of break. Main claim to fame – the school had a beautiful collection of indoor plants, much time having been spent watering them. No stress for her, just for you. Frustration. Lack of direction. Things started but nothing seen through to completion. Did you feel highly motivated? Was there a tangible 'esprit de corps'? Was the school highly regarded? Probably not.

If these two models are flawed, what of the third, the Democratic approach?

■ Democratic Desdemona

This is the model your most recent Headteacher probably sought to emulate. Much in favour with HMI and LEA Inspectors and Advisers. Maximum staff commitment guaranteed by maximum staff involvement, or so it is said. The trouble is that she is so democratic, she can't come to any sort of decision at all! The staff in one school we know became so sick of being consulted about everything under the sun, that in the end they were begging for someone to take a lead and tell them what to do. They left the school in droves in order to work for someone who knew what she wanted.

And therein lies the rub. For like most things in life, the answer is to be found, not in extremes, but in the sensible adapting and blending of a variety of approaches to suit particular circumstances.

■ An objective view of your school

It can be very useful, when examining the effectiveness of any institution, to view it through the eyes of the least experienced recruit. They are likely to have the least biased perception of what is going on. Everyone, even those who don't hold incentive allowances or promoted posts, eventually loses a sense of objectivity, since all members of institutions gradually develop a sense of responsibility, and hence guilt, for perceived shortcomings.

Whilst it is unrealistic to expect your probationer to give a highly critical analysis of your leadership qualities (after all you have still to complete her final report!), I'm sure you found her perfectly happy to provide that list of ideal qualities which ought to be possessed by a Primary School Head.

TIME TO OPEN THE BROWN ENVELOPE

Next comes a humbling experince leading to weaker mortals having a sleepless night wondering what other job they might do!

Your probationer's list probably reads something like this:

'Qualities I would like to see in a Primary School Head'

- Possesses a sense of vision;
- Is committed to the school, its pupils and staff;
- Is perceptive with regard to the needs of others;
- Has a caring attitude;
- Demonstrates a broad knowledge of educational issues;
- Understands people's problems;
- Shows appreciation of jobs well done;
- Finds the time to take a genuine interest in others;
- Offers support when needed;
- Is loyal to staff in times of conflict;
- Comes up with bright ideas;
- Offers firm leadership;
- Is tolerant of weakness and unintentional error;
- Knows when to praise and offer constructive criticism.

Now it is your turn. Compare your list with that of your probationer. How does it measure up?

The likelihood is that your lists are similar. We seem to find it fairly easy to agree on what we see as ideal leadership qualities. The problems arise in our differing perceptions of how effective we are in demonstrating these qualities.

What is also likely to have emerged is at first view a paradox. Your colleague will almost certainly have expressed a desire to work with a strong leader, whilst at the same time expecting that policy decisions will be formulated and approved by democratic process. This is part of a general recognition that complex organisations such as schools must have the committed involvement of all team members, in the making and implementing of decisions, if progress is to be sustained.

There is, however, an appreciation that all effective social, political and business institutions have, without exception, one common characteristic. ONE person leads, encourages, motivates and fires the enthusiasm of the others.

So what sort of leader should YOU aim to be?

■ Try the 3-D approach

Three dimensional people are always the most interesting. The 3-D approach requires leadership to be;

Dynamic
Directed
Democratic

The factors involved in the creation of the most effective primary schools have been investigated in *The Junior School Project* in which, over a period of four years, a team of researchers led by Peter Mortimore, followed 2000 junior pupils through 50 different primary schools. Purposeful leadership appeared to be crucially associated with the effectiveness of schools.

Purposeful Headteachers

- were actively involved with the work of the school;
- understood the school's needs;
- were involved with the staff in curriculum discussions;
- influenced the content of curriculum guidelines without taking complete control;
- influenced teaching strategy;
- monitored teachers' work forecasts;
- emphasised praise of pupils rather than punishment;
- supported and encouraged staff INSET;
- kept track of children's individual progress using class records;
- involved teachers in decision making.

You will now realise why school leadership is so difficult. You need to embrace the most desirable elements of each of the classic 'styles' and blend them together for maximum effectiveness. The most difficult part of this is keeping a sense of balance. Since most of us tend towards one or other of these styles, we have to work harder to promote our least natural characteristics.

■ Leadership has built-in contradictions

There is another problem. You are bound to be disappointed if you believe you can ever acquire all the attributes which make you the 'perfect ' manager. The task is impossible because too many of these desirable qualities are mutually exclusive.

Consider some of the expectations of your probationer:

- You must be highly intelligent yet not too clever.

- You must be forceful whilst being sensitive to people's feelings.

- You must be dynamic but patient at the same time.

- You must be decisive as well as reflective, and so on.

And even if you were to become this paragon of mutually incompatible characteristics, what would happen to the team if you fell under a bus, or were carried off by men in white coats?

■ Does your leadership style enable you to share power?

In the English language, **to manage** can mean to cope (usually with adversity), as well as the finer definitions already discussed. Coping with people and their foibles, their strengths and weaknesses and, most disarmingly, with their variability, is the lot of the leader.

Even if you can resist saying 'It was done this way in my last school' and can combine the charm and powers of a double glazing salesman, you are unlikely to be able to effect lasting changes on a variety of fronts at once. Certainly not on your own.

Newly-promoted Headteachers might do well to reflect on the success of Jesus. Even with divine powers he was frequently misunderstood, disbelieved, and managed to select someone into his inner circle who betrayed him. He was leading a team of twelve.

The way in which a leader goes about the business of instituting change, the disciples recruited, and the distribution of power between them, amount to a leadership style.

Consider the leadership style operating in your own school:

- How do you define your own role in relation to those of others?

- What pattern of communication have you established?

- What procedures have been created to deal with common occurrences?

- Do you demonstrate genuine respect and consideration for the staff with whom you deal?

- Do you act toward colleagues in a warm supportive manner?

- Is this in professional matters only, or does it extend to concerns out of school?

Dimensions of leadership style have been described by Jennifer Nias, amongst others, in terms of structure initiation, decision-centralisation, recognition of situation, model and mission compliance. Each of these factors can be looked at by means of the leadership style checklist below which may lead you to a conclusion about your own style.

Leadership style checklist

- Do you delegate both the task and the decision-taking means to carry it out?

- In which areas of school life does this apply?

- Do all staff feel they are participating?

- Are your actions as Headteacher consistent with the demands of the situation?

- Have you a repertoire of strategies to suit different occasions?

- Do you act as a model of professional behaviour?

- Do you show yourself as well-prepared, a good timekeeper, someone committed to the work of the school?

- Do your words and actions appear to be in sympathy with the stated aims of the school?

The Primary Headteacher is so closely identified with 'her' school, that very often she herself is regarded as the embodiment of the school's mission. This may be resented if staff and others see themselves as the means to someone else's ends. One way in which Headteachers have tried to avoid this, is to embody a philosophy of participation in the school's stated aims. This may be achieved by embracing the ideal of the involvement of teachers, ancillaries and governors, in developing and sustaining an effective school, through their individual responsibilities and collective efforts.

Thus if no individual can combine all these qualities, perhaps a team of individuals can. Let's consider them next.

■ What sort of team have you got?

A team of people is far more than the sum of its individual parts. The most effective team leaders are those who are able to identify and exploit the strengths of their team members. However, we too often classify our colleagues purely in terms of sex, age, subject specialism, coordinator role, etc. In other words, obvious personal characteristics and designated roles.

In an age where collective directed effort, participatory management, continuity of curriculum experience and whole-school approaches to absolutely everything seem to be compulsory, a team working in harmony would seem to be a prerequisite for success. However, if you are going to create a truly effective 'team' rather than a random assortment of individuals who happen to work in the same building, you will need to study how people work best together.

Team role theory was developed by Dr. Meredith Belbin of the Industrial Training Research Unit at Cambridge. The theory is best described in his famous book, *Management Teams: Why they succeed or fail*, and has been convincingly borne out in practice during the past two decades. To achieve collaboration, create a collective will and gain commitment for whole-school policies, it is most important that we should understand how human organisations work, and how we can make them work better.

■ Perfect teamwork

Dr. Belbin's perception is that all members of a team have a dual role. The first role relates to the function that any member plays in the organisation. A teacher is a Deputy Head or Head of Department, curriculum coordinator for maths or science, teacher responsible for Special Needs or whatever.

But the second role, what Dr. Belbin would call the Team Role, is much less obvious. Yet in a sense we have always been dimly aware that individuals play different parts.

Think of your own school. You know that John is good at thinking up bright new ideas whilst Sarah is more capable when it comes to implementing them. You recognise that Sally has a natural tendency to try to grasp control of any staff meeting whilst Graham pours cold water on any proposed innovation. What is more, if John, Sarah, Sally and Graham joined the same Dramatic Society or Golf Club, they would take similar stances in these organisations.

It is these enduring characteristics, these Team Roles, which need to be played in any working group, to ensure an effective outcome. Team members need to complement and balance each other's temperaments and skills.

Selecting new team members

When a vacancy arises, most Headteachers and governors, like other employers, are prone to pick the cleverest and most talented applicant. Unfortunately the most disaster-prone teams are those which are exclusively composed of very clever people.

Over a period of 14 years Dr. Belbin found, in the commercial world, that the most effective teams were those where most, or ideally all of the following team types were present.

While you are reading this next section, try to identify people on YOUR staff who fit into the categories on pages 34/35.

THE CHAIRMAN

The Chairman is not necessarily the appointed team leader. It is important to make this distinction. The Chairman will lead the group subtly and often from behind. Catherine the Chairman is quite free from jealousy, seeing the talents of others as a resource rather than a threat. She operates by clarifying the group's objectives and setting the agenda.

She establishes priorities and thus exercises control over the direction and scope of the discussion.

THE SHAPER

Dominant, assertive, extrovert, impulsive and impatient, Shapers like action and quick results. Sue the Shaper is able to cut through complex issues with pointed phrases and incisive decisions. She dislikes rules and regulations and when operating effectively, commands respect from the others but her abrasive and intolerant manner, however, means that she is fairly unpopular.

Shapers are rather uncomfortable people to have around, but at least they make things happen.

THE INNOVATOR

The innovator has the ability and flair to keep thinking up new ideas which can stimulate and motivate the team. His ideas are distinguished by being original and radical-minded, though not always feasible. He is the most imaginative as well as the most intelligent member of the team. Ian the Innovator frequently criticises the ideas of other members of the team – usually so that he can promote his own. He is markedly poor at accepting criticism himself.

But for all his faults he provides the spark that leads to a breakthrough.

THE MONITOR EVALUATOR

You will not be surprised to discover that Mary-Elizabeth, our Monitor Evaluator, provides the necessary dispassionate analysis of Ian the Innovator's ideas. She is the one most likely to stop the team committing itself to a misguided project. She is the critical thinker whose judgement is rarely wrong, but she has a tendency to be OVER critical and thus be seen as a negative influence who can lower morale.

She may be perceived as being the least motivated team member, but she will stop the team wasting valuable time on impractical ideas.

THE COMPANY WORKER

Christopher, our Company Worker, is the team member who translates theoretical decisions into practicalities and sorts out the jobs for people to do. He is noted for his sincerity and integrity and is not easily discouraged. Give him a decision and he will produce the timetable. Give him an objective and he will produce a chart.

Whilst his consistency and reliability quickly get him promoted to deputy level, he may get stuck there, as his lack of original ideas and leadership skills become more apparent.

THE TEAM WORKER

Tracey the Team Worker is the least visible, but the most vital link in the chain that keeps the team wheels turning. She is very sensitive to atmosphere, and most aware of the needs and worries of others. A likeable, popular, unassertive person, she cements the team together. Tracey's contribution to the team is not highly visible, but if she is absent it becomes very noticeable, particularly in times of stress.

If you have a good Team Worker, give her a treat occasionally to show your appreciation.

THE RESOURCE INVESTIGATOR

Rachael goes outside the group and brings ideas, information and developments back to it. She is sociable and gregarious, and her responses are positive and enthusiastic. She is not as radical as the Innovator, but because of her contacts with the outside, she stops the team either stagnating or losing touch with reality.

THE COMPLETER

Colin always has a sense or urgency. He is anxious and introverted. He is impatient and intolerant of those who are casual and slap-happy. His major preoccupation is with order and he tends to get bogged down with details. He can lower morale in a school, but without him teams can fall behind schedule, make mistakes in detail and simply put things off.

■ How to make use of team-role theory

- Consider each member of your staff in turn. Can you identify their roles?

- Are any of the role types missing? Does this weaken your team?

- Are there too many of a single type? This can produce predictable failure. For example, too many Innovators and not enough Company Workers means lots of ideas but no-one to implement them.

- If a weakness can be linked to team imbalance, can you deliberately alter your own role to compensate?

Our own surveys of around 1200 prospective Deputy Heads, attending our INSET courses indicate a distinct shortage of Innovator-types amongst Britain's primary school teachers. Is this a problem with your staff?

What will you be looking for in the next new member of staff?

REMEMBER, ALL ROLES ARE *POSITIVE* AND *NEEDED* EVEN THOUGH SOME APPEAR MORE ATTRACTIVE THAN OTHERS.

As we have seen, the ideal team will have the right mix of personality types. Complementary skills and talents will be represented, and the age distribution of its members will ensure both continuity and renewal. Real life is of course not ideal. Most of us have to work with what we are given and make the most of it.

A school team needs personalities which interlock to make a workable unit. It also needs leadership to create a shared sense of purpose, giving direction to the work. These leadership functions in primary schools have increasingly been shared through the creative use of curriculum coordination.

During the past 15 years, there has been a growing appreciation of the need to delegate curriculum responsibility. Curriculum consultants (implying specialist expertise) have become curriculum coordinators (suggesting a managerial role) over this time.

■ Curriculum coordinators are your middle management

You need to be clear about the role you expect curriculum coordinators to play in a team of professionals. Here are some awkward questions curriculum coordinators might ask themselves. How would your coordinators reply? Dare you ask them?

- Do I go into other teachers' classrooms to work with them? What reasons do I give teachers for my presence? Am I there as a critical friend; to give an example of good practice in my subject; to discover the quality of the teacher's work in my area or to give advice?

- To whom should I report what I find in other teachers' classrooms? Is this information for my Headteacher, Deputy, governors, SMT or the class teacher only?

- Do all my colleagues have the interpersonal skills to carry out their coordination roles successfully? Do I have any responsibility to help others to gain these skills?

- Am I able to take advantage of management courses as well as those for my particular curriculum area?

- Do I understand the extent of my responsibilities?

- Where is the dividing line between a class teacher's autonomy, and my responsibility? Does my Headteacher play an active role in defining these boundaries?

- What resources can I buy/use without recourse to my Headteacher? Do I hold a budget? Am I responsible for gaining agreement amongst the staff for spending decisions in my area?

- What is the central purpose of the school to which all coordinators, teachers and the senior management team are working?

The way in which the curriculum is managed through coordination is probably the most important indicator of the leadership style of the Headteacher. All the dimensions of leadership are in evidence.

Structure initiation

What nature of decisions can curriculum coordinators make without recourse to the Headteacher? To whom is each coordinator responsible for her managerial role? How is the work of coordination monitored?

Consideration

How much consideration of personal needs and circumstance is demonstrated in the choice and handling of coordinators? What structures are supportive of coordinators (e.g. class-release time)?

Model and mission compliance

Are the coordinators models of good practice in their specialist areas? Is the way in which you encourage, support and advise them on their work a good model for the relationships you intend them to develop with other teachers? Are they enabled to learn management skills from each other? Do both you and they work in harmony with the school's stated aims?

If the participatory aims of the primary school define it as a collective, comprised of teachers, ancillaries, children and voluntary helpers, then curriculum leadership is effectively devolved to each individual teacher. Whether this state of affairs leads to independence or interdependence will depend on the use to which curriculum coordinators are put.

■ Making the most of your curriculum coordinators

During the past decade we have been able to watch curriculum coordination at work in primary schools. In *The Developing School*, Peter Holly and Geoff Southworth show most effectively the factors which leaders in primary schools must consider if they are to make the most of their curriculum coordinators.

* **Get the atmosphere right.**

  Teachers have to be made receptive to a collaborative approach. This may best be done by getting them to respect and acknowledge existing curriculum expertise within their own ranks.
  The Headteacher's task in getting the whole staff to agree the boundaries of classroom autonomy and curricular responsibility is a vital one.

* **Face up to the management implications.**

  Job descriptions should not be too prescriptive and highly

detailed, leaving no room for individual enterprise. Changes have to be seen to benefit the school as a whole rather than merely to advantage the reputation of the Headteacher.

The responsibility for the coordination of the coordinators must be made explicit.

Headteachers need to appreciate the value of reviews and evaluations being done by teachers' peers, rather than just by the Headteacher herself.

Devolution of responsibility will enhance staff confidence, moving them from teacher to educationalist (justifying changes). Headteachers must accept that their own views will be challenged more frequently.

- **Select coordinators with care because their personal qualities are of importance.**

    The willingness of teachers to accept advice depends on their perception of a curriculum coordinator's ability as a teacher, range of experience, ability to organise resources, knowledge of the subject and range of interpersonal skills.

    The relative strengths of curriculum coordinators may determine the priority given to particular subjects in the school's curriculum. It may also affect the resources made available for that purpose.

- **Manage school time with the coordination policy in mind.**

    Time available for curriculum coordinators to do the paperwork will affect its quality.

    Time for curriculum coordinators to work alongside teachers in the classroom is necessary in order to change practice.

    Time to allow curriculum coordinators to see teaching and learning in parts of the school with which she is unfamiliar is required for staff development.

    Meetings must be timetabled to avoid the need to use 'snatched time'.

- **Overcome a role ambivalence.**

    Curriculum coordinators are often reluctant to direct colleagues and enforce ideas.

    Many teachers only accept a coordinating role restricted to writing paper policies and offering tips.

    Coordinators traditionally do not offer comment on colleagues' teaching styles, approach and lesson plans, or act as critical friends. They need to be helped through training to behave more assertively. True whole-school commitment to improving teaching standards would demand this to happen.

- **Ensure appropriate INSET is available.**

Everyone involved has to accept that the nature of this devolved responsibility has moved from curriculum expertise to managerial skill. This means that curriculum coordinators have to be developed in areas such as the implementation of change, curriculum planning, evaluation and school development.
There is a need to help coordinators devlop interpersonal skills.

- **Be prepared to give conspicuous support.**

Success is greater where Headteachers actively support the work of curriculum coordinators. This may involve showing respect, giving extra resources, managing information to this end.
Curriculum coordinators who are asked for regular reports on their work, are more likely to feel that this work is important.

- **Beware of an unbalanced curriculum focus.**

If the only attention given to the curriculum is through curriculum coordinators, then a subject-based thinking will permeate curriculum development.
Emphasis on equal opportunities, IT, Special Educational Needs and other cross-curricular themes, will be weakened unless responsibility for these issues is also included in the school's policy.

Train your middle managers

If your curriculum coordinators are to fulfil effectively all the roles required of them, you must give serious thought to their training.
Since management is predominantly about interpersonal relationships and dealing with people, an initial staff development programme should focus on:

- interpersonal skills;
- effective communication;
- chairing meetings.

■ Interpersonal skills

Headteachers can use whole-school training days to help staff develop awareness of behaviours which will make them more effective in dealing with other teachers. The training day activity – *active listening* has been used most successfully with teachers to raise the issue of the way we listen to each other.

TRAINING DAY ACTIVITY
Active listening

Ask staff to make some preliminary notes about their feelings about their neighbours at home (or any other **tricky** subject). Pair them up and ask that one talks to the other about the way they get on with or how they feel about their neighbours.

After a few minutes ask the teachers to swap roles so that the talker becomes listener and vice-versa.

At the end of this exercise ask each person to note down whether they thought that the listener encouraged them to say more than they had at first intended. Why? The participants should then be asked *'What did the listener do (physical behaviour) to make you feel like this?'*

This should generate a discussion about the listening skills which coordinators need to practise to be effective in their roles. Topics in this area include facial expression, body posture, orientation, head movement and the verbal prompts used to encourage people to talk.

(Further work in this area may be found in Day, Johnston & Whitaker's book *Managing Primary Schools*.)

▪ Effective communication

Some teachers may find that their opportunities to influence colleagues is limited. They may need to appreciate that the method they use to get their message across may be as important as the actual content.

It may help to establish some guidelines for effective communication. The following list is based on the principles in Joan Dean's book *Managing Primary Schools*.

- Teachers need to be addressed personally rather than en-masse.

- The best message is one which rouses interest.

- Information is valued if it is seen to give power or status.

- Notice is taken if a message requires action upon which others will rely.

- It is more effective to use a presentation be it by memo, OHP or verbal, which is appropriate to the intended audience.

- If the source is respected, the information will be deemed important.

- The situation (surroundings, time of day, etc.) should predispose the listener to be receptive.

TRAINING DAY ACTIVITY

Effective communication

Ask teachers to discuss some of these features from the list for effective communication in pairs.

Ask them to relate each area to their own situation and to cite personal examples of both good and bad practice for as many statements as possible.

Join the groups together and get them to establish some schoolwide ground rules for 'Getting the message across'.

Making meetings effective

Meetings are the most common method that leaders use in an attempt to get their message across. They are frequently a disaster! Just having a meeting is not enough. The prime consideration must be *'What do you want to happen at the meeting?'* This point is seldom addressed, for many meetings need never happen at all.

Staff meetings in school

Most primary school staff meetings are to do one of three things:

1 A meeting to communicate information

This type of gathering is typified by having only one speaker (usually the Headteacher) and the information is such that discussion of the decisions involved is obviously unwelcome. Often this information, dates of events, appointments, resignations and promotions, the decisions of other bodies (Education Authority, PTA, governors, etc.), can be given out in written form with only a brief explanation needed, and possibly without having a meeting at all. Wasting every one's time for an hour, to compensate for the Headteacher's lack of foresight in not preparing a briefing sheet, does not go down well with busy teachers.

2 Meetings for discussion

In this case, participants need to have been properly prepared beforehand by being given the relevant information. The seating arrangements can be used to encourage participation. A brainstorming session recorded on tape can generate ideas or possible solutions.

The key to success for this type of meeting is to create an atmosphere which encourages staff to share ideas and perceptions. They will not do this if early statements (however foolish) are not accepted as starting points for the generation of further ideas.

3 Meetings where decisions are to be made

Everyone must be made aware that the meeting has this purpose. Time has to be allowed beforehand, such that small group meetings can already have aired some of the issues.

Printed material should have been read and absorbed. Teachers should know whether a vote will be taken if necessary, or whether the debate will continue until a consensus (or exhaustion) is reached.

■ Running a staff meeting

Coordinators will be helped to understand the difference between the various purposes of staff meetings. This process may best be started by instigating discussion about the various behaviours stimulated by different types of meetings.

The list below was produced by a group of teachers who wanted to improve the quality of their meetings in school. It could be used as a starting point for other teachers.

CHARACTERISTICS

POSITIVE	NEGATIVE
Well-chaired	Leaving important issues to last
Humour to break the ice	Interruptions
Agenda previously circulated	Agenda too large
Keep to the point	Unattainable objectives
Relaxed atmosphere	Dominated by a few people
Good minuting	Personal attacks
Time limits adhered to	Inconclusive end
Aims are clear	Consistent non-participation
Respect shown for all viewpoints	
Positive outcomes and agreed action	
Focus on few items at a time	

You may then invite staff to consider strategies for organising and chairing meetings. Their aim should be to ensure that as many as possible of the negative features are avoided and the positive ones achieved.

Meetings also have another purpose in the primary school. By passing the chairmanship around, Headteachers can demonstrate a commitment to the participatory ideals expressed earlier. They can allow coordinators to experience skills which they will need to develop if they are to rise through the ranks. They can allow the strengths emanating from the team roles possessed by the group, to ensure achievement through collective effort. Headteachers can show in public the value they place on the skills of their staff, by occasionally taking a back seat.

In short, meetings allow leadership not only to be shared, but also to be seen as shared.

▉ Conclusion

This chapter has been aimed squarely at you, the Primary Headteacher. Others reading it will doubtless extract from its pages ideas which will help them analyze the management styles and structures of the establishment in which they work.

Remember:

- Work towards being a '3-D' manager.

- Be aware of the team roles operating within your staff group and make use of team-role theory when appointing new staff.

- Assess the functional roles of the school's middle management – your curriculum coordinators.

- Provide a training package to enhance the skills of these middle managers.

- Make the most of communication as a management tool.

4 Making the most of your Deputy

'The worst job in teaching......'

'I felt like the meat in a sandwich......'

'most difficult and frustrating four years of my life......'

Three fairly typical responses from newly appointed Headteachers, reflecting upon their periods as a primary Deputy. Not a very satisfactory reaction to what should be one of the most creative and stimulating periods in a teacher's career.

So what has gone wrong?

This chapter:

- examines the current role of the Primary Deputy Head;
- challenges the suitability of this model;
- offers some effective alternative roles.

The current role of the Deputy Head in the primary school

In 1944 the McNair report first recommended that there should be Deputies in primary schools.

The Burnham committee made these posts mandatory ten years later. The Houghton pay awards established independent pay scales for Deputies and, more recently, Deputy Heads have seen their pay linked to that of Heads rather than to that of the rest of the profession. However, despite this long gestation period, a universal definition of the Deputy Head's role recognised by the whole of the education community has yet to emerge.

▓ What do Deputies do?

In order to analyze the current role played by primary Deputies, we might start by looking at just what Deputies do. Between 1988 and 1991, aspiring Deputy Headteachers attending courses with the authors, were given the following instructions:

▶ **'One focus of the course is an examination of the role of the Primary Deputy. Please prepare in advance and bring with you a list of the functions and duties performed by your Deputy. It is important that this list of jobs describes what your Deputy actually does, not necessarily what you believe the role of the Deputy to be.'**

Course members then worked in groups to produce three lists:

- List one identified those tasks which were common to all schools represented in their group, i.e. total unanimity, all Deputy Heads did these things.

- List two was similar but allowed for one exception to complete consensus.

- A third list was constructed of all those remaining tasks performed by some Deputies but not by others.

The teachers found themselves surprised by the results of the analysis. Most groups struggled to find any tasks or functions which were common to Deputies in all the schools in their group. From 100 such groups none came up with more than three common tasks. On the other hand, the number of one-off tasks was overwhelming. One teacher commented that it appeared that every Deputy in England and Wales seemed to have a different job.

An analysis of the data collected from approximately 750 schools suggests the following:

Nearly all Deputies:

- deputise for the Headteacher in his/her absence;

- take some assemblies;

- organise hall timetables and duty rostas.

Many Deputies:

- are used by the Headteacher as a sounding board;

- liaise between the Headteacher and staff;
- teach a class;
- enforce discipline;
- chair some staff meetings;
- maintain contact with external agencies;
- supervise students;
- act as a curriculum coordinator.

And there the consensus ceased!

Scores of other duties were being performed by Deputies across the country, but with no evident pattern.

These included:

- responsibility for School Fund
- INSET Coordinator
- capitation allocation
- lunchtime organiser
- prospectus editor
- teacher governor
- minuting meetings
- requisition/stock
- visits coordinator
- arranging supply cover
- reviewing forecasts
- etc. etc.

The list was endless and included some more obscure activities, a favourite being:

'Chasing the horses from the field!'

This very significant variation and lack of consensus as to what constitutes a Deputy Head's role came as a great surprise to many course members. They generally assumed that the situation existing in their own school was typical.

The unifying factor – Non-managerial tasks

Apart from the large **variety** of the tasks performed, the other noticeable feature is their mundane and routine nature and the general absence of managerial responsibilities. Few of these tasks help the Deputy to develop a whole perspective, or gain skills which will subsequently be needed for Headship.

Why have Headteachers, the major role definers, sustained this situation? Perhaps because the duties are so very boring and routine. They are all jobs which obviously need doing for the school to function. If the Deputy were not to perform such chores, someone else (probably the Headteacher) would have to. The most common response made by our course members to this finding was to re-label the Deputy Head as 'Dogsbody Head'.

This lack of consistency in role definition has some alarming implications:

- What meaningful training can be given beforehand unless the principal ingredients of the role are common knowledge?

- How can recruitment be satisfactory unless the selectors share a common perception of the work required?

- How can common selection criteria be applied to applicants' level of success in their present job when all the jobs are so different?

This situation does not appear to be new. Commentators have cited the problem of the Deputy Head's lack of precise job definition over a number of years.

The 1978 HMI primary survey found a more significant role being played by curriculum post-holders than by Deputies.

And Patrick Whitaker notes in his book *The Primary Head*:

▶ **'In practice what Deputies do ranges between carrying out a few administrative chores at one extreme to a full association with school policy-making at the other.'**

This is supported by Alan Coulson's research *'What do Deputies DO?'* which found the whole area of the Deputy Head's role to be surrounded by anxiety and uncertainty.

▶ **'Despite his nominal status the Deputy is likely to be overburdened with petty tasks and teaching than to be deeply involved with important issues concerning the school as a**

whole. This emphasis fails to make use of the Deputy's knowledge, skill and experience.'

Nor do the 1988 conditions of service appear to have helped to redefine the Deputy's job. Paragraph 32 defines the Deputies' special contribution:

- *Assist the Headteacher in managing the school or such part of it as may be determined by the Headteacher;*

- *Undertake any professional duty of the Headteacher which may be delegated by the Headteacher;*

- *Undertake, in the absence of the Headteacher and to the extent required by the Head or the relevant body . . . the personal duties of the Headteacher.*

▓ The management team

The demands on school managers are manifold. Few individual Headteachers can be expected, singlehanded, to be financial administrator, personnel manager and curriculum leader.

What is the range of duties which fall to the school's managerial team? Just a few are itemised below. Many are legally binding upon the Headteacher and cannot therefore be prioritised away.

- Ensuring effective teaching of the Programmes of Study required for each NC subject;

- Ensuring that each subject is adequately and appropriately resourced in order that individual Attainment Targets can be met;

- Establishing appropriate recording strategies for NC subjects;

- Meeting the challenge of achieving NC requirements through a thematic approach;

- Revising schemes of work when appropriate;

- Establishing and managing a Records of Achievement scheme;

- Managing an appraisal system;

- Marketing the school;

- Regularly reviewing and updating the school development plan;

- Implementing policies approved of by the governors with respect to sex education, admissions policies, acts of worship, charging, etc.

- Establishing a system for providing written reports to parents;

- Monitoring the implementation of regulations relating to hours of schooling, religious education, etc.

- Administering NC assessment programmes;

- Governor training;

- Servicing governors' meetings and sub-committees;

- Selecting staff, in conjunction with governors.

And with Local Management:

- Budget planning;

- Budget analysis and monitoring;

- Advertising for and recruiting staff in a shrinking market;

- Day-to-day routine maintenance.

This list is by no means exhaustive but gives some indication of the managerial load to be carried within the school.

It is therefore inevitable that primary Headteachers must either delegate some of their responsibilities or fail to meet the challenge of this decade. This is a stark but uncompromising choice. They must learn to delegate a part of their traditional role or they will fail the school and in turn the children they are committed to serve. Primary Deputies can play an important and rewarding part.

Such a concept of corporate responsibility and professional partnership has both appeal and danger. It involves true delegation and joint ownership of the leadership function in primary schools as a prerequisite to the achievement of a school's curricular aims and objectives.

The demands of the National Curriculum, including its implications for the assessment and recording of pupils' progress, coupled with the fundamental changes brought about by LMS, make it imperative that Headteachers review and reconsider their own roles. This gives a context to sharing the management of the school in partnership with the Deputy or Assistant Head.

> DON'T FORGET THE CHILD!
> THE NEED FOR A CURRICULUM LEADER

It's worth reminding ourselves at this point, just how important the 'Curriculum' aspects of school management are.

Ask teachers to focus on the purpose of schooling and their thoughts centre on the attitudes, skills, concepts and knowledge that children will acquire in school and will carry with them throughout their lives.

Providing an optimum learning environment must be our prime management mission. We must not allow ourselves to be distracted from that.

■ Effective school management

The importance of active and purposeful curriculum leadership, has been highlighted in Jennifer Nias' work *Leadership styles and Job Satisfaction in Primary Schools*, published in 1980. She examined the work factors associated with teachers' job satisfaction and established that these mainly stemmed from their perception of the effectiveness of their teaching and the value Headteachers put on this. Headteachers who were disengaged from the teaching process, where children's learning and teachers' standards were not monitored, and where other matters occupied their time and attention, were associated with schools where children made less progress and where teachers derived very little job satisfaction.

> ACTIVE CURRICULUM MANAGEMENT IS ESSENTIAL TO
> ACHIEVE OUR PRIME MISSION

The tasks involved in curriculum management might be considered as an amalgam of:

a) Curriculum oversight, once the traditional preserve of the Headteacher –

Maintaining an overview of the work of the school and ensuring coherence, reviewing teachers' forecast books, ensuring breadth, relevance and continuity, setting up the school's curriculum review cycle.

b) Assisting the curriculum coordinators in –

promoting good practice in separate subject areas, monitoring

NC coverage, keeping up to date with recent developments, acting as local adviser in specialist areas, etc.

c) A response to statutory requirements placed upon primary schools e.g. managing assessment, organising moderation and administering statutory reporting to parents.

■ A valuable role for the 'Assistant Head'

If the curriculum is to be effectively managed as outlined above, and all other aspects within the non-curricular sphere to be maintained, a management partnership of Head and Assistant Head may provide the answer.

Such a management partnership is most effective if the totality of management responsibilities are divided equitably, bearing in mind the Headteacher's responsibility for the school, and her sensitivities.

An analysis of such areas might include the following:

CURRICULAR	NON-CURICUULAR
Curriculum management	Staffing and personnel matters
Team Leader – Curriculum coordinators	Policy-making
Pupil assessment	Links with Governors
Record keeping	Liaison-community interests
Overview of teachers' planning	Marketing & public relations
Evaluating quality	Financial administration
Curriculum development planning	Whole-school review
Whole-school curriculum review	Monitoring quality
Records of Achievement	Contacts with parents
Administration of NC testing	LMS delegated powers

The management partnership might share these responsibilities in a variety of ways, to suit the abilities and inclinations of the people concerned. Some items might, of necessity, need to remain within the orbit of the Headteacher, e.g. monitoring quality and policy-making. Nonetheless, at least four alternative management models become immediately apparent.

MODEL A
The Headteacher as Director of Finance and Administration
Assistant Head as Director of Curricular Studies

MODEL B
Headteacher as Director of Curricular Studies
The Assistant Head as Director of Finance and Administration

MODEL C
A compromise position between A and B above with the Headteacher and Assistant Headteacher assuming a mixture of responsibilities within both fields.

MODEL D
A new appointment to be made, with a role equivalent to bursar, leaving the Headteacher and Assistant Headteacher to work in much the same way as now. (See Gittins 1989.) In smaller schools a bursar would need to be shared between a cluster of schools, perhaps spending one day per week on the finances of each of five schools.

■ The role of the Assistant Head as Director of Curricular Studies

The Deputy is closer to the teaching process than is the Headteacher. Certainly in all but the very largest schools this is because the Deputy has a class of his or her own. Even where this is not the case, the Deputy usually has more teaching duties than the Headteacher, acting as cover in case of illness, classroom relief for curriculum coordinators, taking groups with special needs, etc.

This inevitably precludes the Deputy from assuming some management functions. For example, it would be difficult to be the principal agent for parental liaison; to deal with certain LMS/financial matters and to get out into the community to develop the necessary links, whilst shouldering a full-time class-teaching commitment.

It is also impossible to maintain an overview of the day-to-day progress of the school constrained within the walls of one classroom, as many Headteachers, who have in the past committed themselves to an overambitious teaching timetable, have found to their cost.

However, this situation may be turned to an advantage when it comes to some tasks associated with curriculum leadership. Comments such as *'I'd like to see him try to do it at the same time as teach 34 children'* or *'I sometimes wonder if she's ever been a class teacher'* are not infrequently aimed at innovative Headteachers. The charge that ideas cannot be put into practice is difficult to make against a teaching Deputy whose own classroom speaks louder than words. A partial solution may lie in arranging for some classroom cover to be given to the Deputy.

The issue of the deployment of teaching staff within a school, has been raised in a number of articles by Norman Thomas (esp. ILEA 1985). His guideline is a simple one. If an additional member of staff reduces the class size to below 35, then careful consideration should be given to alternative uses of that teacher. Releasing the curriculum manager to enable him/her to carry out some of the duties above may be one such use.

If, therefore, the management of the design and delivery of the curriculum is the focus of the school's most important function, who better to lead that process than the Assistant Head, a classroom practitioner of repute. The Deputy's frame of reference will certainly be classroom work. This is to her advantage. How could this be achieved?

1   Curriculum leadership

In most cases, we have found that the Deputy currently appears to carry a curricular responsibility. In doing so, she is able to demonstrate leadership skills by showing the way this duty is best discharged. It is the task of each Deputy to abstract from the features of her own role those elements which can be universally applied. Acting as a model is a particularly appropriate technique for Deputies to promote quality curricular management practice. Even where it is not felt to be appropriate for the curriculum manager to also be a coordinator in one particular function, a need will arise for temporary stewardship (in the case of staff resignations/ secondment, for example). In these cases the above arguments will also apply.

In terms of evaluating progress, the team leader will have a duty to review curriculum devlopment plans, ensure that proposals match the school's overall development plan and undertake, with individual coordinators, evaluation processes to assess progress. Personal characteristics the Deputy would need to succeed in this area are a freedom from jealousy and an ability to generate a high level of trust.

2   INSET

We have found many Deputies, in partnership with the Headteacher, willing to be involved in managing the staff INSET arrangements. Individual teachers' needs, as identified through curriculum coordinators' reports or a whole school review exercise, might be met by intelligent use of the INSET budget. Whole-school training day activities would be guided by the Deputy who, by the same means, would have developed an overall grasp of the school's curriculum strengths and weaknesses. Control of the INSET budget would allow the curriculum manager to best use this knowledge.

3   Continuity and records

The processes and means of curriculum continuity and record-keeping need to be decided by agreement amongst the teachers concerned. The Deputy, as a fellow teacher, would have the most credibility to lead the discussion and monitor the resultant decisions. Communication and interpersonal skills are at a premium here.

4   Curriculum resources

Under LMS, resources for classroom materials, subsumed under global budgets, may well be threatened by more immediate demands. If Headteachers and governors are under pressure to have repairs done, to augment the heating allowance, to pay extra for a scarce teacher, to fund increased telephone or photocopy charges, then there may be a temptation for the new set of reading books, or the world studies programme or the LOGO chip to be put back just one more year.

It will be essential to protect curriculum resourcing by disassociating its budget from the rest of the school's spending at the very start of each financial year. The high status of the Assistant Head as Director of Curricular Studies would be a major safeguard, enabling initiatives to be funded in line with priorities in the school's curriculum delivery programme. The professional judgements made would then be based on intimate knowledge of the teaching work of the whole school.

5   Staff meetings

Many Deputies are already practised at organising and running effective staff meetings. Gaining the cooperation of teachers through their engagement with issues by this means is vital to managing the curriculum. The sensible use of this meeting time has become an issue in some schools which adhere rigidly to 1265 hours. Meetings have to be not only properly managed but seen to be properly managed. If the general routine staff meetings, consisting of selecting dates for events; discussing issues relating to general school policy; responding to PTA requests and the like were timetabled for only a set proportion of such meetings, the rest of the time could be programmed to furthering the aims of the curriculum under the leadership of the Deputy. Such a distribution of meetings in an eight week half-term might be:

week 1	Full staff meeting admin, etc.
week 2	Curriculum focus – music
week 3	Curriculum focus – geography
week 4	INSET reports from teachers attending courses
week 5	Full staff meeting, admin. and discussion on discipline/school image
week 6	Curriculum focus – cross-curricular themes and dimensions
week 7	Moderation meeting – NC progress rewiew
week 8	Curriculum focus-theme planning for next half-term

Meetings in weeks 1 and 5 would be led by the Headteacher, others organised by the Deputy (although meetings in weeks 2, 3 and 6 would be led by appropriate subject coordinators).

■ Deputy Heads' responses

Working groups of Deputies from across the United Kingdom considered this management model during a series of our courses.

The following observations highlight some of the conditions for making the model work and its potential advantages and disadvantages, as they perceived them.

Prerequisites for success

- Teaching Deputies would have to be given a significant element of class non-contact time (which currently many do not get).

- Governors must be convinced of the necessity/advantages of the new management structure to persuade them to fund the extra staffing needed.

- The Headteacher must be committed to true delegation of specific aspects of his or her traditional role.

THE ADVANTAGES

1 Because roles are clearly defined and published, staff appreciate to a greater extent the work done at management level within the school.

2 In the eyes of LEA, governors and parents, the curriculum is clearly in the hands of the school.

3 The Headteacher is able to offer a dispassionate view of the work of the school. She can be far more objective about the quality of its outcomes, not having her reputation on the line as part of the curricular planning and process team. Such an arrangement allows Deputies to assume more of a managerial/supervisory role adding to their experience and enhancing their promotion prospects.

4 The adoption of this pattern of responsibilities releases the Deputy from low order 'servicing chores' allowing other staff to see the needs of the school at this level.

5 The Deputy has an opportunity to demonstrate leadership qualities (and to learn from her mistakes).

6 This type of organisation relieves the school of having to employ a bursar whose judgements may be, or may appear to be, financially rather than educationally driven.

7 The Headteacher is prevented from assuming that the school is just an extension of her own ego, and ignoring the Deputy.

8 This form of management structure involves a much greater commitment on the part of the Deputy Head than at present. This may be used as a lever over time to raise the salary and status of the position.

THE DISADVANTAGES

No management strategy is ideal, and some disadvantages to this particular plan have been identified. The main concern expressed by practising Deputies was the fear of being distanced from the financial and administrative functions of management. They considered this to be a potential disincentive for any Deputy who was ambitious for promotion to Headship.

Two responses may be made to these concerns:

The Deputy who wishes to remain a Deputy

There are many Deputies who are content to remain as Number Two in the team. They are frequently people with outstanding pedagogical expertise whose real forte is the practice of teaching. For them, to be designated Director of Curricular Studies, with real powers and responsibilities, would be a crowning summit of success. There are many who embarked on a career in teaching because they loved the rewards of working with children, not because they wanted to be education administrators. These people have often been undervalued in the past by professionals and public alike. They have also suffered anxiety, guilt and a sense of personal inadequacy because they have not wanted to go on to Headship.

The role of Assistant Head/Curriculum Leader would enhance their own self image and raise their standing in the eyes of the rest.

The Deputy who seeks Headship

Deputies who are ambitious for Headship do need to remain in touch with the realities of Financial, Administrative and personal matters. The solution for them might be a policy of 'Job Swaps' with their Headteacher.

A number of opportunities arise from such an exchange of roles:

- Temporary job swaps could be seen as part of an apprenticeship scheme to which future Headteachers would be entitled.

- Job swaps of this nature would ensure that the vast experience of Headteachers is not lost to the profession and that curriculum leadership is not the poor relation in this management partnership.

- Further job swaps over a period of a term or so would prevent either partner from becoming blinkered in their somewhat restricted role, and also prevent staff from viewing the Headteacher as 'remote' or detached from the process of teaching and learning.

◼ Conclusion

In examining the current role played by primary Deputies and by exploring ways in which that role may be redefined, we have identified a major problem – that of Role Conflict. No other post held in schools requires the occupant to resolve so many conflicting demands.

- Where does the Deputy's ultimate loyalty lie? It is with the Head, with the staff, with the parents, with the governors?
- With all the other demands being placed upon him, how can a Deputy meet the most commonly expressed expectation, that he should be a model classroom practitioner?
- If he devotes himself to a curriculum leadership role, will he reduce his chances of promotion to Headship?

Pradoxically, despite these difficulties, Deputies hold the key to the future. As we have argued elsewhere, few Headteachers are able to cope alone with the increased workload which is involved in managing the primary school of the 1990s. Failure to delegate is the most common barrier to school improvement. Where a true partnership based on mutual trust and respect is created, the possibilities are infinite.

It is the clear duty of every Headteacher to give careful consideration to these issues, since by enhancing the status of her Deputy she will create a more effective management partnership for the benefit of all.

5 Better management by negotiation

Some readers may consider it curious to include a chapter on negotiation in a book on school management. After all, most teachers probably think of educational 'negotiation' as taking place outside the school setting – for example between unions and the LEA.

In fact, negotiating permeates the fabric of our everyday lives to such an extent that we are hardly aware of its existence. But it is taking place, all the time, both in school and elsewhere. Before examining negotiation within the school setting, let's consider some of the occasions when we need to negotiate. Remember, negotiating is not always about price. Terms and conditions, or simply an agreement about how to proceed, may be of even more importance.

Some real life negotiations

- Agreeing a price to have a repair job done on your house;
- Deciding with your partner where to go on holiday;
- Prioritising expenditure within the family budget;
- Coming to an arrangement with a neighbour regarding boundary fencing;
- Agreeing the time your teenage daughter should come home from a party!

The key factor to remember is that negotiations do not need to have winners and losers.

John Lockett writing in *Be the Most Effective Manager in your Business*, suggests that successful negotiators must always remember the:

TWO GOLDEN RULES

NEGOTIATING IS A TECHNIQUE OF BARGAINING IN WHICH TWO PARTIES ATTEMPT TO REACH A MUTUALLY ACCEPTABLE AGREEMENT.

WINNING A NEGOTIATION IS ONLY POSSIBLE IF BOTH SIDES
ACCEPT THE FINAL OUTCOME.

■ Negotiations in school

Negotiation occurs whenever two parties have a slightly different perception of a situation and expect slightly different outcomes, yet want to come to an agreement. It should therefore be evident that effective teachers are negotiating almost continuously. Good teaching requires constant negotiation over a whole range of issues. Teachers who aim to rule imperiously invariably fail. Those who negotiate terms and conditions with their pupils usually succeed. It is the element of respect for the other's viewpoint and needs which is the critical factor. Good teachers respond in this way without realising it.

Now re-read the preceding paragraph and substitute HEADTEACHER for TEACHER and STAFF for PUPILS.

Does it still make sense? Of course. The qualities that enable effective teachers to get the best out of their pupils, equally apply to the effective management of staff. This is why we are able to predict with a reasonable degree of certainty that a good teacher will make a good Head. The skill of people-management, whether with children or adults, is all to do with interpersonal relationships. Ability in this area is related to a significant degree with an individual's powers of bringing negotiations to a mutually satisfactory conclusion.

Repeatedly, Headteachers are required to draw upon these powers to deal with everyday school situations.

The following examples give an indication of the range of activities which are likely to involve negotiations:

- Meeting with teachers to draw up job descriptions;

- Counselling a recalcitrant pupil;

- Deciding on the balance of responsibilities between you and your Deputy;

- Meeting with a parent to attempt to resolve a grievance;

- Prioritising targets with colleagues;

- Dealing with sales representatives – schools with delegated budgets are increasingly being targeted by companies for direct selling.

In addition there will be more formal negotiations with governors, not the least about your salary arrangements.

■ The negotiating process

We have established that effective teachers have developed negotiating skills and honed them to near perfection through years of practice. Why then do so many, when faced with a pushy sales representative, feel uncertain – even inept? The answer usually lies in the unfamiliarity of the situation.

The key to successful negotiating in an unfamiliar setting is to understand the structure. Many people imagine, when dealing with a salesman, that the discussion is a wholly spontaneous affair. If the salesman has been particularly effective, the customer will leave the showroom believing he has won the bargain of a lifetime.

In reality few professional negotiators are 'playing it by ear'. Most have been carefully trained to proceed in a very specific manner. Many companies have detailed sales manuals which identify every move a customer might possibly make and offer the appropriate counter thrust. The key to successful negotiating in an unfamiliar setting is to understand the structure of the negotiation process. If you can appreciate what is going on and have some knowledge of the tactics being employed, you will have a better chance of being able to shape and direct the outcome of the negotiation to your advantage.

It is equally the case, that a knowledge of Negotiation Theory will enable you, as a manager, to arrive at solutions to the typical school situations which were outlined earlier.

■ Process and strategy – Let's play the Negotiation Game

Negotiations are not processes of logic, like a game of chess. Participants bring with them emotions and prejudices which can upset the best laid plans. There are, however, a number of ground rules which apply to all situations, and these must be understood before we may proceed.

Guiding principles

- The most effective negotiators are those with clearly defined objectives and a well-thought out strategy. The most fatal mistake is to attempt to 'play it by ear'.

- Detailed listening to your opponent is vital. You can only hope to make progress if you understand his objectives.

- Constructive arguments will pay dividends. Don't lose your temper!

- Don't give things away – trade them.

- If you have high aspirations, you will achieve more than if you play safe and only aim for what seems realistic.

In order for any negotiation to succeed there must be scope for agreement. This area is often referred to as the 'Middle Ground'.
This can best be presented diagrammatically as follows:

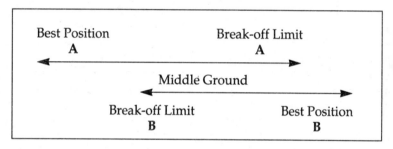

In the diagram, the bargaining takes place in the 'Middle Ground' between the limits which the two sides set themselves.

If there is an overlap here, then there is scope for negotiation. Each side will have their 'Best Position,' which is their ideal goal. It is equally important to have a clearly defined 'Break-off Limit', beyond which it is preferable to end negotiations rather than settle beyond that point. Of course, the bargaining may not just involve one factor, e.g. price, but may include a range of other elements, for example a free-service contract, which could be traded off in order to reach an agreement.

The bargaining model in action

We can flesh out the bones of this model, with an example taken from school.

Headteacher Maureen and Deputy Head Jane are about to meet to negotiate the amount of non-contact time which will be provided to enable Jane to undertake the additional duties of Curriculum Leader.

Headteacher Maureen feels sympathetic to her Deputy's case, but there are several restraints on her generosity:

- She only has 0.5 of a teacher without a class and she is engaged on essential remedial support work.

- To release her Deputy, Maureen will almost certainly have to increase her own teaching timetable. She is not keen on this because the school has a delegated budget and there is much she is uncertain about.

- She knows that the Deputy is not over popular with the staff, who believe that the extra salary already paid to the Deputy should mean extra 'work' not extra 'free time'.

Maureen's Best Position is to grant a maximum of 10% class non-contact time (1/2 day). Her break off limit is 40% (2 days) but this would cause major strains.

Deputy Jane is looking forward to assuming the new role of Curriculum Leader, but doesn't see how it can be done effectively without significant class non-contact time. She needs time to:

- be able to monitor National Curriculum implementation;

- work alongside colleagues;

- deal with additional paperwork, review teachers' forecasts, etc.

- review children's work;

- undertake classroom observations;

- enhance her status as Deputy Head.

Jane's Best Position is to seek 50% class non-contact time (2 1/2 days). Her break off limit is 20% (1 day), but she believes this would seriously jeopardise her ability to be effective.

Whilst it is evident that the 'Best Position' of the participants (10% for the Head, 50% for the Deputy) are wide apart, there is an overlap providing the scope for agreement.

Using our diagrammatic model, this can be seen quite clearly:

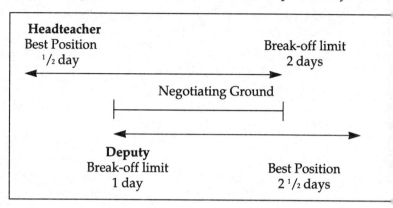

The bargaining ground is now clearly defined as being between one and two days.

What strategies should each of our negotiators employ to maximise their chance of arriving at an agreement which is closest to their own 'Best Position'?

Strategy

We are now ready to examine the classic stages through which all effective negotiations should proceed. They do not always follow in strict sequence but can be observed in most negotiations as follows:

- PREPARATION
- PRESENTING
- LISTENING
- ARGUING/CLARIFYING
- BARGAINING
- AGREEMENT

Preparation

The best negotiators prepare in detail for the meeting. One of the most important aspects of preparation is to decide on a 'Fall-back Position'. This is a half-way stage between the 'Best Position' and the 'Break-off Limit', and reduces the chances of being driven back to the

Limit, which may give time for recovery.

The essential elements of good preparation therefore are:

- A clear view of your interests and aims. What is your *Best Position*?

- A realistically set limit to your negotiating options. What is your *Break-off Limit*?

- A pre-determined Fall-back Position in case things begin to go badly wrong.

- An appreciation of what your opponent is likely to want from the negotiation. What is his Best Position?

- A carefully researched estimate of the least he is likely to settle for – yet still feel a sense of achievement. *This is not necessarily his limit.*

TWO GOLDEN RULES

NEGOTIATING IS A TECHNIQUE OF BARGAINING IN WHICH TWO PARTIES ATTEMPT TO REACH A MUTUALLY ACCEPTABLE AGREEMENT.

WINNING A NEGOTIATION IS ONLY POSSIBLE IF BOTH SIDES ACCEPT THE FINAL OUTCOME.

John Lockett's Golden Rules cannot be stressed too frequently in the context of school-based negotiations. If a negotiator beats her opponent down to her limit, she may have 'won' the battle, but will ultimately lose the war.

Negotiating in the workplace is not like buying a car, where the two participants need never see one another again after the sale is concluded. The Headteacher and Deputy in our earlier example have to continue to work together each day, and to respect each other as professionals. If Maureen were to force Jane back to her Break-off Point and use her position as Headteacher to impose an ungenerous settlement, relationships might well be soured in such a way as to influence Jane's whole attitude to her role as Deputy. It is clear that great delicacy is required in such situations.

■ Presenting

This is the first stage of the Bargaining process. It is your opportunity to present your case clearly and without interruption. At this stage you should be setting out your case very clearly. Your opponent must be in no doubt as to your objectives. There are three main rules to be considered:

** Be Positive **

By presenting your case positively you will show that you are confident and well prepared. If you are nervous or tentative in your approach, you will be giving your opponent a big advantage.

** Be Precise **

Much time can be lost in negotiations because of the use of woolly and ambiguous language. When presenting your case be crisp, precise and accurate. At a later stage in the negotiation, you may deliberately use a vague expression to signal your willingness to move on a particular point. But not at the outset.

** Be Polite **

Nothing is likely to be gained by a hot-tempered, bad-mannered approach. An angry negotiator is a potential loser. Remember our 'Golden Rules' and think about tomorrow!

It is worth mentioning, however, that a brief outburst of controlled anger, if planned, can be a useful ploy. When President Kruschev of the Soviet Union banged his shoe on the table in the United Nations, he was actually still wearing shoes on both feet! The 'spare' shoe had been brought along deliberately. Prime Minister MacMillan's cool response 'Can we have a translation of that?' was a perfect example of how to diffuse tension through humour, whilst demonstrating that he was neither impressed nor intimidated.

■ Listening

Listening is the counterpart to presenting. Depending on the particular negotiation you may present or listen first. You should be aiming to listen actively and make use of your opportunity to weigh up your opponent's Best Position.

Note principal points. After you have listened carefully, start asking questions. It is important that you explore all aspects of your opponent's case and fully understand his objectives. Don't stop until you are quite certain that you have a firm grasp of his position.

During this questioning phase, be particularly careful to listen for signals. 'Signalling' is the way effective negotiators suggest the possibility of movement or compromise.

'*The governors are unable to agree to your request for Performance Related Pay at this stage*', means '*depending on what you are prepared to concede, then PRP could be on the agenda later.*'

▦ Arguing

This is the centre ground of the negotiation between Presenting / Listening and Bargaining / Agreement. This is when a first stab is made at challenging the unacceptable elements of your opponent's case. A key skill here is summarising. By playing back to your opponent your interpretation of what you think he means, you may be able to gain his agreement to a subtle change of emphasis which can be used to your advantage.

▦ Bargaining

We are now in the most important part of the negotiation process. Through listening, questioning, arguing and summarising, you should be fully aware of your opponent's position. You will now be ready to move towards a solution.

> BARGAINING IS THE PROCESS OF TRADING THINGS YOU
> HAVE FOR THINGS YOU WANT.

As Headteacher you are concerned about the amount of teaching time being lost during the afternoon session, because of breaks. Although playtime is officially only 15 minutes in duration, a more realistic figure is nearer to 30 minutes, when winding down the first lesson, cloakroom times, lining up and settling back to work factors are included.

You decide that the only solution is to abolish afternoon break, but obviously you need to carry your staff with you. Not unreasonably, they will see this as a significant alteration to their conditions of service, and as such a matter for negotiation. They may well have sympathy with your objective, but will probably seek concessions in return. If they give up their break, what arrangements will be made for a mid-afternoon drink? How can a class be covered if a teacher needs to respond to a 'call of nature'? As the afternoon session is from 1.00pm to 3.30pm., may individual teachers take their classes outside for a five minute break if this will aid concentration? What about the usual school rule that older children should not normally go to the toilet during lesson time?

Concessions over these or other issues may be the means to achieve your objective and retain the goodwill of your staff.

■ Agreement

The closure of negotiations is a question of fine judgement. The longer you continue, the greater the concessions you may achieve, but equally you may have to make. In the end both sides are likely to sense when 'enough is enough'.

If agreement cannot be reached – a likely outcome if there turns out to have been no overlap or bargaining ground between the break-off limits of either side – then closure will occur without agreement. This is an unwelcome step, but as Headteacher you may consider it preferable to making unacceptable concessions.

In order for there to be final agreement, the solution must be acceptable to both sides. To achieve this your final offer must be credible and acceptable.

Credible because your opponent must believe you can be pushed no further.

Acceptable in the sense that it takes account of your opponent's aims.

If your final offer is unacceptable, you may still win grudging acceptance because of your opponent's poor bargaining position. If this happens, he is likely to hold it against you and wait for an opportunity to get his revenge.

When agreement is reached, have it written down to make sure the terms and conditions are crystal clear.

It is important to send a written summary to your negotiating partner so there can be no argument at a later stage.

Always remember that, whilst as Headteacher you can invariably impose your wishes, to do so may irreparably damage relationships, and ultimately your ability to effectively direct colleagues. As a last resort, of course, you have the right to impose a soundly-based decision. How much better, however, to trade away one or two concessions which are of little importance to your main objective, whilst retaining the goodwill of your staff.

All too frequently Headteachers, teachers, governors, elected members and Education Officers see negotiaton as a battlefield rather than as an area of opportunity. When effectively handled, negotiation can enhance mutual respect and understanding, leading to increased confidence and trust.

■ Local Management – the negotiation challenge

Local Management of Schools significantly increased the number of occasions when Headteachers need to negotiate directly with others. Individual Headteachers, with particular requirements to satisfy the needs of an individual school, can negotiate prices, balanced against terms and conditions, to achieve maximum benefit. At least those who know something of how to negotiate can do so.

Therein lies the challenge. As established contracts for school meals, grounds maintenance, cleaning of buildings, etc. expire, new ones must be negotiated. Whilst negotiating new or revised contracts may be a glorious opportunity for the confident and experienced, it can be a nightmare for the unwary. Governing Bodies will have an important role to play here. Far-sighted Headteachers will ensure that at least one governor (coopted if necessary for the purpose) will be an able negotiator with a business background.

In most instances, of course, the Headteacher will always be the front line negotiator. A case study may be helpful here. Let's examine the acquisition of a new photocopier using the negotiation model already discussed.

■ Preparation

Send for brochures. Decide which machine you want, which add-on facilities are desirable, how much you can afford to pay, what your Fall-back Position will be. Check with other local schools how much they are paying. Consider alternatives to rental; purchase with service, leasing, etc.

Fix date for Rep to call.

■ Presentation

You begin by presenting your case – outlining your needs, the price you hope to pay, your interest in the possibility of a lease arrangement rather than outright purchase and any other questions to which you need answers.

■ Listening

The Rep now gives you his sales pitch. Don't forget to question and listen for signals. You may explore the scope for flexibility at this stage and proceed with the negotiation. Alternatively you may thank him for his demonstration and request time to think the matter over. You will need to do this if you are considering a number of different suppliers.

■ Arguing

Challenge any weak or conflicting information you have been given. Don't forget to summarise. Push against initial assumptions that the catalogue price is fixed and the agreement conditions inflexible.

■ Bargaining

The Crunch!

He offers the 'super GT' model at the full-lease price, but is willing to include a free two-year service agreement.

You know from your research that this service agreement is standard practice so he is giving away nothing. You tell him the price is far too high and that you want free service for the full term of the lease, i.e. five years.

He says he can't alter the price because that is fixed by his bosses – he could, however, plead with them to include some 'adds-on' free of charge.

You are quite keen on this. You wanted a document feeder and sorter/collator on your machine, but had originally decided against it on grounds of price. You don't show your pleasure, however, but do imply that things are looking a little more promising.

He now resorts to a fairly common ploy and asks to use the phone so he can consult his boss. He says his boss is unlikely to agree, but that he will do his best. He is most likely to want to use the phone in another room if one is available. Before going he will summarise the wonderful deal you are getting if only he can manage to swing it.

You wait patiently. He may know that you know what he knows! That this is all part of the game. However, he can't be sure. You prepare for the next stage which is going to be critical.

He returns to the room (or puts down the phone) and beams with relief. He informs you that despite all odds he has persuaded a reluctant boss to agree to your terms. If the phone conversation has taken place within your earshot, it will no doubt have been a dramatic tour de force, worthy of an 'Oscar'.

You nod graciously but wear a worried frown. In his absence you have checked your figures and realise that his price is still 0.1p per copy more expensive than the deal offered by his competitor company, whose Rep was in yesterday! However, you like the 'super GT' and if he can match the price, he has a deal.

He caves in.

So he has an acceptable deal above his limit, or he would have closed without a sale. You have got the machine you wanted at the price you had negotiated with his competitor company, but with free peripherals and an extended service agreement. You are both happy because the outcome is mutually acceptable.

■ Conclusion

Effective managers need a range of clearly defined skills. Amongst the foremost of these, is the ability to negotiate successful agreements with a variety of people and agencies. The only real way to learn to negotiate is to do it - and then coolly analyze the results of your endeavours. Through such an analysis you can learn valuable lessons for the next time.

- Was my preparation thorough enough?
  Did I clearly define my Best Position?
  Was my estimate of my opponents' limit realistic?

- Was my presentation crisp and concise?
  Was I positive?
  How did I handle any aggression?

- Did I listen actively and pick up signals which I was able to use?
  Did I take notes which were helpful?
  How much movement came about because I summarised to my advantage?

- How effective were my bargaining ploys?
  Did I give too much away without gaining something in return?
  On balance did I 'win' or 'lose'?

- Do I feel satisfied with the final agreement?
  Is my opponent likely to feel satisfied with the outcome?
  If not, why not?

Only by being honest with yourself will you do better next time. Armed with the skills of successful negotiation, you will be equipped to become a formidable force within your school.

6 Appraisal – a partnership of endeavour

Schools have no commodity to sell to the local community other than knowledge and skills. The workforce through which they do this is teachers. To improve the quality of that workforce we need to enhance opportunities for work planning, to develop teaching skills and to maximise the quality of support for members of the teaching team. Performance appraisal is used in business as a means of achieving these objectives. This chapter examines its application to schools.

What is appraisal?

- A structured process of regular reviews of achievement as a background to forward planning.

- For the individual teacher; a periodic examination of professional duties, career development and job satisfaction; and an opportunity to give feedback on the school and the way it is run.

- For the school; a continuing means of developing the full potential of the staff.

Performance appraisal of teachers has been developing over a number of years and under a variety of labels. These have included school-development programmes, staff development and review initiatives, INSET needs identification, etc. Whatever the label, the purpose has been to assist teachers in focusing on particular aspects of their work in order to bring about improvements in performance.

Of course it can be argued that performance appraisal has always been with us as a profession. Isn't it the case, that each time the Headteacher visits a teacher's classroom a judgement is made about that teacher's performance? If the teacher subsequently applies for a new job, will not these judgements be reflected in the written confidential reference which the Headteacher is required to provide?

A clear case can therefore be argued for an open system of performance review. In such a system the criteria and parameters of the review are known and agreed by both sides, the procedure is laid down clearly and unambiguously, judgements which are made and conclusions which are drawn are minuted, recorded openly and agreed upon by both appraiser and appraised.

This must be better than a system which relies upon 'behind the scenes' methods of assessment and reporting; of subjective judgements unsupported by evidence; of telephoned references involving oblique innuendo.

It is evident from the reaction of many in the profession, that it is possible to view appraisal from two alternative perspectives. The process can either be seen as being positive and developmental in nature or be perceived as negative and threatening. It is understandable that many teachers should be wary and sceptical, feeling that appraisal is less about enhancing good performance and more about identifying and punishing weakness.

The way forward must be to allay these fears by accentuating the positive and developmental aspects of the process. Given the right framework, procedures and process, teachers can come to see an annual performance review as a right to be preserved, with a variety of benefits for the individual.

◼ The 'whole-school review' approach to appraisal

A first step in emphasising the importance of positive appraisal is to include individual performance review within the scope of the whole-school evaluation.

Seen within the context of school development planning, staff appraisal is linked with the growth of the school as an institution. The key is partnership. Schools have been referred to as 'communities of endeavour': how better to extend teachers' own professionalism than to encourage them to share responsibility for the growth of their school by participating in an effective management process.

◼ Make your aims positive

In his book *Grey Eminence*, Bob Spooner points out one of the pitfalls in carrying out appraisal interviews:

▶ **'One of the difficulties.......with any appraisal system is to discover those elusive qualities which the best teachers have in abundance, which they display in the security of the classroom, but which may be masked by some glaring but inconsequential weakness.'**

It is clear that our aims must be stated very clearly and positively:

- Appraisal must be positive, creative, and developmental and must celebrate success.
- It should recognise teacher autonomy in the planning, organisation and evaluation of the appraisal process itself.
- It should aim to identify and build on strengths and successes.
- It should affirm teacher's individual strengths, enhance their place in the staff team, and build self esteem.

Appraisal has purposes which support both teachers and schools:

For the teacher

- Appraisal can assist in clarifying a teacher's role within the school through a clear job description.
- Properly conducted, regular appraisal, will enhance professional relationships, by giving the teachers a real sense of being listened to and valued.
- An objective review of current performance undertaken in a positive atmosphere can enhance a teacher's self image.
- Target setting (and the monitoring of progress towards those targets) gives a sense of purpose. This is where the offer of support needs to be unequivocal and guaranteed.
- Assistance with career development should be part of the appraisal process.

For the school

- Appraisal will encourage schools to discuss and clarify their objectives.
- A process which identifies many areas ripe for development will force institutions to determine priorities.
- All schools have strengths and weaknesses. Appraisal will assist in identifying where development is necessary.
- Because performance appraisal is about teaching, it will provide evidence needed for a study of curriculum management issues.
- Appraisal within the context of the whole school review, will identify INSET needs and enable a planned programme of staff development activities to be provided.

Appraisal techniques

Your LEA may issue guidelines regarding who will appraise whom. There will certainly be a policy regarding the appraisal of Headteachers and this may extend further. Much will depend on the size of the school. In a small school of five teachers, or fewer, the Headteacher will need to appraise each member of staff unless there is good reason not to do so. In a medium-sized school it is a good idea for the Headteacher and Deputy to share the role of appraiser, in a medium-sized school the Headteacher might appraise the senior management team who will then in turn share the appraisal of the rest of the staff.

Self appraisal

Before the formal process of appraisal takes place, teachers should undertake a systematic analysis of their own performance. This can be best achieved by providing a questionnaire which encourages self review. The following is an example of one such approach.

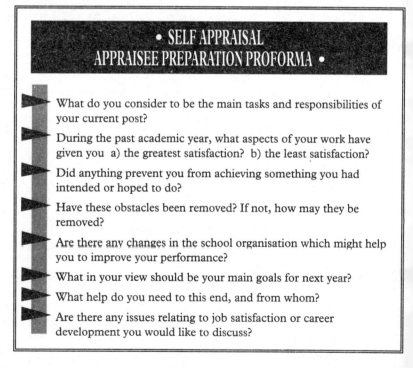

• SELF APPRAISAL
APPRAISEE PREPARATION PROFORMA •

What do you consider to be the main tasks and responsibilities of your current post?

During the past academic year, what aspects of your work have given you a) the greatest satisfaction? b) the least satisfaction?

Did anything prevent you from achieving something you had intended or hoped to do?

Have these obstacles been removed? If not, how may they be removed?

Are there any changes in the school organisation which might help you to improve your performance?

What in your view should be your main goals for next year?

What help do you need to this end, and from whom?

Are there any issues relating to job satisfaction or career development you would like to discuss?

■ Classroom observation

This is a most important part of the process. If the subsequent appraisal interview is to be founded upon classroom practice, then the appraiser must have had the opportunity to observe the teacher in action. A major focus for the appraisal interview is the performance of teachers in the classroom. Observations can be general or specific in focus. It can be diagnostic in purpose or emphasise monitoring or evaluation issues. It must be clear to both appraiser and appraisee what is being observed and how this is to be carried out.

In addition to providing objective data on actual performance, this will enable the appraiser to get a feel for the teacher's style and relationships with the class as a whole.

It will also give the appraiser a clearer view of the challenges and difficulties facing an individual teacher within the context of his or her day-to-day working environment. A pre-meeting needs to be scheduled during which agreement is reached regarding the lesson which will be observed, the objectives the teacher has determined and the particular aspects of the teacher's work which will form a specific focus for later discussion.

■ Classroom observation checklist

Pre-meeting

Which lesson will be observed?
What activities will be taking place?
What are the teacher's objectives?
What pupil activities are planned?
What outcomes are expected?
When will the observer join the class?
What role will the observer play?
How will the observer make notes, etc?
By what criteria will the teacher's work be judged?

■ Establish the criteria for good teaching performance

It is important that both the observer and the observed are aware of the criteria by which the observed lesson is to be judged. This may be done at the pre-meeting or would valuably form the basis of a training day activity.

TRAINING DAY ACTIVITY

What makes a good teacher?

The aim of this exercise is to get teachers to develop agreed criteria against which classroom performance may be judged.

Divide staff into appropriate groups to come up with a list of teacher behaviours which would be indicators of good teaching. It might be easier to start with the idea of writing a report on a mythical student on teaching practice. Ask, '*What would the class teacher look for when assessing the student's classroom performance?*'

When each group has reported back, use their ideas along with your own, to create an agreed observation schedule as appropriateness for staff with different age groups of children.

◼ Observing teachers in the classroom

Arising from the pre-meeting or from a training day exercise such as the one suggested here, an observation schedule should emerge.

This might include:

- Planning, preparation, suitability of learning objectives, organisation of resources, relation to school schemes of work and the National Curriculum;

- Teaching skills and techniques, effectiveness of lesson start, interactions with pupils, balance of explaining and instructing, questioning and appropriate use of language, organising pupil groupings, record-keeping techniques and classroom layout;

- Management, control and relationships. Timing of pupil activities, management at start, of pupil movement, of individuals, of groups. Control of entry/exit to room, use of rules and routines, vigilance and awareness, use of praise, rewards and encouragement. Working relationships and rapport with pupils, enthusiasm and confidence;

- Ability to analyze own performance.

Teacher's forecasts and records

In order to put a single classroom observation session into context, you will need to review the teacher's forecast and planning document. It is best if this is an extension of good practice, where the appraiser regularly reviews teachers' planning documents as a matter of routine policy. Reviews of teachers' work-plans may be undertaken at intervals varying from weekly to termly. The most common practice is for teachers to plan in half-termly blocks and for their forecasts to be reviewed half-termly.

The appraiser should also look at the children's assessment records and work portfolios in advance. This will ensure that the observer has a 'feel' for the class group and the levels of attainment which may be expected. It is important that teachers do not feel threatened by this process. An appraiser who gives the impression that she is nit-picking and looking for faults or inadequacies will quickly erode the teacher's confidence. This will influence the validity of the observation and may jeopardise the opportunities presented by the whole appraisal process.

Tact and sensitivity are paramount.

The interview

If the appraisal is to be taken seriously throughout the school, the interview must be given high status and should be arranged at a convenient time with at least two weeks' notice.

Tell the school secretary not to allow any interruptions other than in a genuine emergency. Arrange the furniture in a welcoming and non-threatening manner, and make sure tea or coffee is available. The atmosphere should be efficient, professional and egalitarian.

Running the interview

- Begin by describing the appraisal process, and outline the structure of the interview. This provides security and confidence.
- Ask the appraisee to analyze her own performance, starting with everything she is pleased with. Give plenty of time to this part of the interview. Agree where you can, and add your own list of possible achievements and qualities.
- Remember the 80% rule. LISTEN and EMPATHISE for 80% of the

time. Many interviewers find this difficult to stick to.

- Open-ended questions will encourage the interviewee to express their own ideas. Use them.
- Become an active listener. It is your responsibility to hear and understand the appraisee's position. Ask for further examples summarise the main points and keep prompting until you understand the position precisely. Summarising should always take place at the end of each section of the interview.
- Don't forget the importance of appropriate body language.
- Encourage the interviewee to analyze and reflect upon what she would like to have done better. This is an important part of helping her to identify her own solutions to the problems which she herself has identified.
- Do not respond too quickly. Suspend judgement and let silences occur.
- Direct criticism can be quite intimidating. Positive reinforcement of correct attitudes achieves the same results more effectively.
- Use evidence gained from the classroom observation session as a starting point for your discussion and as a point of reference for particular examples.
- Maintain the appraisee's self esteem. Avoid being too judgemental. Encourage the interviewee to make self-analytical comments.
- Remember that if there is a problem with her performance, the problem is yours as well as hers. Try to find ways of tackling it cooperatively.
- Work towards agreed outcomes. These will form the basis of the statement of intent which is written down at the end of the target setting stage of the interview.

▇ The interview structure

While there are a number of alternative ways of structuring the interview, any successful scheme will include the following:

- A review of successes, achievements and performance against previous targets;
- The identification of areas for development;
- Some clearly defined and agreed targets for the future.

A successful interview will have a clearly defined format which is agreed beforehand. It will consequently be less threatening, since the interviewee will know in advance what to expect. It will also pay you to ensure that the questionnaire your teachers used for preparation (page 78) covers the same ground as the interview and preferably in the same order.

It can be helpful if the interview commences with a discussion of whole-school issues rather than immediately tackling an individual teacher's performance. Beware, however, of being distracted into school controversies instead of concentrating on individual performance.

Let's work through one such model structure and see how it works.

Introduction - Outline of the meeting

Although the structure of the meeting will have been agreed upon and discussed in advance, take the opportunity to open the meeting and 'break the ice' by recapping on how the interview will go.

STAGE ONE – THE SCHOOL
Strengths
Areas needing development

STAGE TWO – PERSONAL PERFORMANCE
Successes and achievements
Aspects of performance requiring development
Specific target setting

STAGE THREE – CAREER DEVELOPMENT

The School

Ask the interviewee to open the discussion by itemising what he considers to be the principal strengths of the school as an institution. This will provide a welcome opportunity for a little self-congratulation which can be a positive and encouraging start to the meeting. Move the discussion on to an analysis of those areas in which the school needs further development. Refer to the School Development Plan and elicit opinions as to the ordering of priorities.

Having listened actively, draw this section of the interview to a close by summarising ideas. Stress the positive by emphasising how valuable it would be to implement some of the appraisee's suggestions and agree to take forward his ideas to the Head / governors / SMT for further consideration.

Personal performance

Open this important part of the interview by once again accentuating the positive. Ask the interviewee to identify what he considers to be his major successes and achievements during the period under review. Press for evidence which demonstrates that the initiative has been successful. Encourage a declaration as to what he thinks others see as his strong points. This is a good strategy for encouraging people to talk about themselves with less embarrassment.

This stage provides for the natural progression which leads to an examination of the aspects of his work requiring attention and improvement. Invite him to reflect on these areas and to try and identify ways forward.

Be aware that the most effective way of persuading a teacher to adopt policies for self improvement, is to encourage him to generate his own strategies. Throughout the discussion constantly encourage the interviewee to find ways forward and to identify solutions. With a strategy agreed, invite him to consider which area he considers to be the priority for personal development. Agree what support would be most approrpiate in order to assist him in meeting his objectives.

Conclude by summarising the main points of the discussion and arrive at a consensus with regard to specific targets. These will be captured in writing at a later stage.

Career development

The interview concludes with a session designed to provide appropriate advice and support regarding the devlopment of career objectives.

Appropriate documentation will be needed:

- to record achievement;
- to structure preparation.

For both appraiser and appraisee:

- as a focus for discussion;
- as a record of agreement of   a) what is said.
                                  b) the targets agreed.

Your appraisal will fail if:

- remedial action is not offered to remedy perceived weaknesses in performance;
- either party is allowed to be bland or superficial and render the process ineffective;

- unachievable goals are set;
- one party is allowed to dominate the process and only quasi-agreement is produced.

Follow up

The appraisal interview must not be seen as the end of the process. The first and most immediate phase of the follow-up procedure must be to write down the agreed targets for development, together with a clear statement of support which will be provided in order to assist the teacher in meeting the agreed objectives. Though some ideas have been presented, other support strategies might include the following:

- Discussion with other teachers or observation;
- Advisory service provision;
- Involvement in decision making;
- School-based INSET;
- Change of role or additional responsibility;
- Rotation of responsibilities within school;
- Teaching partnerships;
- Improved communication;
- Exchange of information;
- Revision of job description;
- Secondment and/or exchanges.

Finally, the process of implementation needs to be regularly monitored and evaluated during the months which follow. Without regular evaluation and subsequent development monitoring, the whole process will fail. Not only will this be very wasteful of the time and effort put into the process thus far, it will also lead to disenchantment, cynicism and reluctance to participate in future appraisal activities.

The most effective way of ensuring success, is to build in a predetermined timetable for review which involves the teacher in the evaluation process. With this principle retained at the heart of the monitoring process, much can be achieved.

Always remember that to be successful, appraisal must be positive and developmental. If we can retain these as our guiding principles, we should be able to look back at our early faltering steps, and wonder how we ever managed without such a basic management tool.

7 Managing with money

■ Budgetary control

As head of a Locally Managed school you have to ensure that an effective system of budgetary control is in place. You will need to decide who is to control and monitor spending, ensuring that resources allocated to various budget headings are being used effectively.

Most schools will have a Finance sub-committee of governors which will meet at frequent intervals, and which will report to the full Governing Body at its termly meeting. Even so it will be your duty to service the committee and to provide the necessary information and guidance which will assist them to arrive at the best decisions. Never underplay your experience and professionalism in this context. Remember that most governors are unfamiliar with the detail involved in the running of schools. This does not reflect badly upon them. It is exactly as it should be. You are the Managing Director. They are the Board representing the shareholders. In the vast majority of cases, Headteachers find their actions applauded and their recommendations confirmed.

What then are the regular budgetary control tasks? To some degree the actual detail will vary from LEA to LEA, depending upon the Management Information System which has been installed in your school. The following assumes the most common pattern, which is a personal computer station in the school linked to a mainframe computer at some central location within the LEA. The most flexible systems allow direct access into files held in the Treasurer's Department, Direct Works (building maintenance) and the Parks Department (grounds maintenance).

The most satisfactory way to monitor expenditure is to establish a procedure which will provide the time to undertake the following.

Reconciliation

Each week you will need to reconcile the information held on your school PC with that on the mainframe. This is a simple process which results in a printed list of transactions conducted since the last reconciliation.

The suspense file

Not all transactions will have been reconciled. Perhaps an invoice number has been keyed in incorrectly. Or perhaps a charge for a supply teacher made on the mainframe cannot find an appropriate match on the school's PC. This may be because the school has failed to input the supply teacher's details on their PC. It may be because the supply teacher actually worked at a different school! The suspense file system is the means of catching this sort of error. The system is most effective, since only expenditure which has been originated or approved on the school PC can be charged to the school budget. All other items (those held on the suspense file) must be individually checked before being either rejected or cleared for payment.

Financial reports

Having undertaken your weekly reconciliation and cleared as much of the suspense file as possible, you can now call for a set of financial reports. The precise details of these will vary from system to system, but should provide information at a number of levels of detail. One of the most popular programmes is provided by SIMS in their LRM package (Local Resources Management). It offers the following structure:

A   Overall school budget share

B   Main budget headings:

      employee expenses
      educational materials and equipment
      repairs and maintenance
      energy
      other premises expenses
      transport related expenses
      communications and fees
      miscellaneous expenses
      income

C   Budget accounts within main budget heads
e.g. for employee expenses:
    teaching staff
    ancillary staff
    supply staff
    hourly paid staff
    other employee expenses

D   Department accounts
These are departments set up to suit individual requirements, for example within the educational materials and equipment budget account.

For each layer within the structure of budget headings used in your system, up-to-date financial information is available.

Let's take as an example the repairs and maintenance of premises account.

Initial budget allocation

This is the total amount of money which has been allocated for minor repairs and maintenance of the building. You will need to be familiar with your local scheme, to check that items which are the responsibility of the LEA (usually major repairs, roofing problems, etc.) are not accidentally charged to your delegated budget.

Expenditure to date

Orders placed and invoices received for work completed. The system is likely to offer a range of detail shown as:

    Orders placed but invoices not received;
    Invoices received but not processed;
    Invoices processed and passed for payment;
    Invoices paid and account reconciled.

Running totals of expenditure cleared through the system, together with orders placed but invoices yet to be processed will give:

Budget allocation variance

The amount of money remaining after all expenditure, both cleared and in the pipeline, has been deducted.

◼ Detailed examination of financial reports

There may also be included a comparison with a hypothetical expenditure profile. For example, if the money for building maintenance (say £3,600) was divided on the profile into equal twelfths (£300 per month), the financial report would indicate that by the end of month six, £1,800 should have been spent. If the work undertaken has only cost £1,300 to that date, the computer will show a saving on budget of £500, and project that to the year end. These projected under and overspends need careful monitoring as they can give totally false figures leading to unwarranted optimism or panic.

It is unlikely that you will wish to print comprehensive sets of financial reports each week when you do the mainframe reconciliation. You will want a complete range of reports to present to your finance sub-committee at their meeting. This will not only keep them informed and interested, but will also provide the information which you will need to support any case you may wish to put as the year proceeds, for transferring funds from one budget heading to another. This is the principal role of the finance sub-committee, other than operating as an audit section. For example, projected savings on the gas bill may allow an extra classroom to be refurnished before an end of year price rise takes place.

◼ Budget planning

One of the most important tasks to be undertaken is that of planning the next year's budget. In fact the £300,000 or so which constitutes the average primary school budget is much less of a challenge or an opportunity than might be imagined. Once fixed staffing and premises costs have been deducted, precious little remains. However, whilst few may wish to be over creative or adventurous during their first year, confidence will soon grow as experience is acquired. Effective Headteachers will in any event have involved their Deputies in this process (many Deputies, if not formally governors in their own right, have been coopted on to Governing Bodies), so a newly appointed Headteacher should not be starting off from scratch.

Your Local Authority will have provided a structure which will be set up already on the computer. Your task is therefore relatively simple, and consists of allocating money to each of the budget headings. In some cases – such as for staffing costs – you will be informed how much to allocate in order to cover your existing staffing establishment, plus a figure for anticipated salary increases. In others, for example energy costs, you will have historical data with which to work. You will know how much your fuel bills were for the previous year and will need to increase this to cover anticipated price rises. Fixed price contracts will exist for some items – perhaps grounds maintenance and window cleaning.

It is the balance remaining, when all these unavoidable commitments have been met, which provides the flexibility and choice which LMS was set up to promote. Savings can definitely be made on a small scale by in-house economies but to make a major financial investment, for example to undertake a large scale redecoration programme, or to replace floor tiles or some other costly improvement, will involve serious decisions being made regarding staffing levels. It is here that the governors have their real role in deciding whether to postpone replacing a teacher in order to pay for redecoration, new furniture or some other capital investment.

These will be the unpopular/no-win choices which have to be made. It is quite proper that those who have been elected, or who have accepted nomination to 'govern', grasp this particular nettle and do not attempt to vacillate in the face of difficult decisions.

■ Staffing considerations

It is in the area of staffing where the most significant decisions are likely to be made, not only with regard to the number of teachers employed, but the balance between experienced staff and new recruits. It might be tempting to employ an abundance of probationers at the expense of more experienced teachers at the top of the National Scale and thus make significant savings. It is here that market forces begin to operate. With more open enrolment within the primary sector, parents have more freedom regarding their choice of schools. Governors who sacrifice more experienced staff in order to make financial savings could soon pay the penalty in popularity, finding the school roll falling as parents vote with their children's feet! This in turn would reduce income as formula funding fell. A spiral of decline could quickly become established which would be very difficult to reverse. Funds also need to be set aside for the employment of supply teachers. Most LEAs make provision for the cost of long-term supply cover from centrally held resources, but cover for short-term absence will be financed from the school's own budget. To reduce this cost to the minimum and release money for other purposes, you may decide to organise to provide a full time 'floating' teacher – one without class responsibilities. This may be relatively easy in a large school, but in a smaller primary will only be achieved at the cost of larger classes. The point at which the trade off between larger classes against a floating teacher becomes unacceptable, is a matter of judgement. Again, parents as well as teachers may find over-large class sizes unacceptable, especially if a neighbouring school operates with significantly smaller classes.

■ Salary levels

Governing Bodies have the following discretion with regard to the salary levels for teachers:

- Headteachers and Deputies may be paid at any level within a salary range relating to the size of school;

- The number of Incentive Allowances can be varied within a discretionary range;

- Special discretionary payments – incremental enhancements – may be paid to individual teachers;

- The Governing Body may extend the normal salary scales for teachers.

Governing Bodies can use these discretionary payments to enhance recruitment, retention and motivation of staff. Governors may feel conflict between allocating a larger share of the school budget in this way and spending the money in other areas (books and equipment for example). On the other hand, you might argue that the most important resource available to the children is the staff. Providing an adequate salary structure to reward outstanding commitment and achievement must therefore be a top priority. Failure to do so will lead to the most able teachers seeking employment elsewhere where their talents are suitably appreciated. This is a very delicate issue, for the parents who will initially complain that money should not be spent on teachers' pay when it could be used to buy new furniture or computers, will soon change tack when the best teachers begin to leave the school to take up better paid jobs elsewhere.

You may need to be well prepared in advance of making these points to your governors, so that you do not appear simply intent on self advancement, providing the justification for a much higher salary for yourself.

■ Coping with the extra work

Whatever the advantages of managing your own budget, and they are many, there is no doubt that it is demanding of your time and energy.

If Primary Heads attempt to maintain their traditional workload and simply add on the extra burden of a delegated budget, then they will fail. This will affect the whole quality of education offered by the school, for the single most significant factor influencing the success of a school, is the effectiveness of its Headteacher. Strategies need to be devised which will prevent this from happening.

The KEY is to be able to REVIEW, PRIORITISE and then DELEGATE.

■ First review your role

The first step is to review your own role. This can be done in a number of ways and a combination of the following approaches may achieve the best results:

- Write down a list of all the jobs you do as part of your role as Headteacher. Include even the most insignificant chores which you have to perform.

- Go through last year's diary, day by day, drawing up a list of all the activities undertaken, organised or led by you, which you have recorded.

- Work out a rota of children (perhaps from the local high school) to work-shadow you for a week. This will be an interesting experience for them in addition to making you acutely aware of the interruptions to which you are subjected!

- Ask your Deputy to compile a list of the duties he/she thinks you perform. Ask one of your least experienced teachers to do likewise. You are likely to see yourself portrayed in a quite different way from your own perception.

■ Now prioritise

Having amalgamated the results of your various approaches to gathering information, you should have an extensive item bank of duties and responsibilities which constitutes your role as Headteacher. Of course they are not all of equal importance so the next step is to prioritise. This can be done by either **rank ordering**, i.e. arranging the items in a continuous list, with the most important first through to the least significant last. This is relatively easy at the upper and lower ends of the scale but it becomes very difficult to differentiate between items towards the centre. Alternatively the items can be handled by **banding**. The number of bands may be between three and five. In a three-band system items would be grouped as follows:

Band A   Place in this band all items which are crucial to the effective performance of Headship. Any Headteacher who failed to undertake these duties would be guilty of dereliction of duty. The effectiveness of such a school would be seriously undermined.

Band B   List here duties and jobs you perform which are not contingent upon your position as Headteacher, but which you do because of personal choice; because no one else will do them; because you have previously felt guilty about asking anyone else to do them; or for any other reason.

Band C   Contains the items which remain. Band B items tend to be in the grey zone. Whether these are crucial to the performance of effective Headship will be open to personal interpretation. External factors will also affect this, for example the personalities and abilities of the individuals concerned; the type of school and its catchment area; etc.

It will be in sorting Band B items that the perceptions of others can be of most assistance.

Give your list to the colleagues who assisted in its compilation and ask them to undertake the banding exercise.

The extent to which their decisions coincide with yours will tell you much about the match of your perception of your role and how they see you. Be prepared for a shock!

A further refinement of the above is to apply a five-band system. Items are arranged as before but into five bands thus providing a more detailed analysis, particularly of the centre ground.

▉ It's time to delegate

You will now have a clearer view of the relative importance of the vast number of jobs you perform. If you are to function at a peak of efficiency, and in doing so maximise the effectiveness of your school, you must reduce your workload by delegation.

A pre-requisite of this is the creation of effective senior and middle management teams by creative use of the Incentive Allowances which are at your disposal.

Band A items: Must be done by you.

Band B items: Most may be done by you but some will have a training function and could be shared with your deputy.

Band C items: Delegate as many of these as possible.

As we are concerned in this chapter with Financial Management, specific consideration must be given as to whether all aspects of Financial Management fall within Band A. Chapter 4, which considers the role of the Deputy, has a contribution to offer to this debate.

■ Delegating financial delegation!

There are a number of options open to Headteachers who feel confident to delegate some aspects of budgetary control to others, whilst retaining overall responsibility:

- Enhance the role of the Deputy to 'Assistant Head – Finance Director' (See Chapter 4).

- Create a senior staff Finance Team to mirror and service the governors finance sub-committee.

- Take advantage of any financial skills existing within the Governing Body – perhaps a co-opted governor who is a banker, accountant or works in finance.

- Buy in the services of a Bursar.

- Enhance the status of the school secretary, encouraging her to assume more responsibility for the weekly reconciliation and review procedure. This will have cost implications to finance regrading and/or increased hours.

The Bursar option is not as farfetched as it may seem, even for the average-sized primary school. Any of the options outlined above will have 'cost' implications with the exception of the Volunteer Governor. The cost may not be financial but may be measured in work hours not being spent on other priorities. If curriculum development or delivery is adversely affected by time spent on financial management, then a cost factor is definitely involved.

A Bursar employed by a consortium of 10 schools, spending just half a day in each on rota to undertake the weekly reconciliation and review, and to trace and clear the suspense file queries, would be money very well spent.

■ Conclusion

Local Financial Management has proved to be one of the most positive elements of the 1989 Education Reform Act. With strategies for the delegation of some roles and responsibilities as outlined above in place, the extra workload is manageable. The additional opportunities and flexibility given to school managers can make their work much more satisfying.

We believe that this trend will continue. Schools will become increasingly independent of Local Authority influence. *The Parents Charter – you and your child's education* published by the DES in 1991, lays further emphasis on the choices available to both parents and schools. The concept of regular reports provided by teams of Independent Inspectors could further erode the powers and functions of the LEA.

8 Using pupil assessment to improve teacher performance

Introduction

Assessment is an essential and natural part of the teaching process. Primary teachers have always assessed their children in some way or another, for assessment is at the heart of good teaching.

If the assessment process is to be effective and to the benefit of children and their schools, it must be properly managed. Schools and teachers must consider carefully the ways in which they assess and record their children's progress. They will need guidance and leadership in this. The benefit to your school and its pupils will be that you will be able to improve the delivery of the curriculum, whenever weaknesses are revealed.

You will need to address a number of assessment-related issues and to develop and adopt whole-school policies for them:

- A school assessment policy;
- Curriculum planning and assessment;
- Teacher assessment in the classroom;
- Managing standard assessment tasks;
- Record-keeping procedures;
- Reporting procedures.

Each issue, in its own way, offers an opportunity for teachers to examine the effectiveness of the teaching and learning taking place in their classrooms. The essential task for schools must be to ensure that the assessment process has value and meaning for its children and their parents, and that the school's curriculum and methodology does not become assessment led. It is therefore crucial that you have a well thought-out, coherent philosophy of assessment embodied in a whole school policy. As you create such a policy you will have opportunities to examine current teaching practices, re-inforcing the importance of the needs of the child at the centre of the learning process.

■ Some principles for a whole-school assessment policy

1 Clarify the purposes of assessment.

The first stage will be to consider the school's purposes for assessment.

Assessment can be:

Formative: able to lead on to further learning and growth; able to help teachers identify the next step in that process;

Summative: a statement of a position which has been reached at a particular point in time;

Evaluative: capable of being used to evaluate the learning activity or wider curriculum plan which led to the assessed position;

Informative: giving understandable information about the person assessed.

It is essential to determine the relative emphasis to be placed on these different elements, and for the school as a whole to share a perception of why assessment is taking place. This is the first step in formulating a clear policy.

For example, you might have identified three main reasons for assessment:

- To assist the learner in the process of learning;

- To assist the teacher and subsequent teachers of those children in the planning of learning through the curriculum;

- To inform those whose right it is to know about the performance of their children.

You will need to decide what it is you need to assess in order to fulfil each of these purposes.

2 Decide what to assess.

You may do this alone or with the senior management team, but it is most effective if you can involve the whole of the teaching staff. One means to this end would be to use the following training day exercise or something similar.

TRAINING DAY ACTIVITY

Purpose of assessment

Divide staff into four groups and give each two sheets of A3 paper. Each group is to discuss and report back on their conclusions to the two questions you have given them from this list:

1 What do we need to know about the children in our class?
2 What would parents like to know about the school performance of their children?
3 What information does the next teacher need to have in order to teach her classes as effectively as she can as soon as she can?
4 What do children need to know about themselves in order for them to best benefit from their schooling?

This session works most effectively when each group does not know the nature of the other groups' questions until the plenary session. The aim of this exercise is to gain some agreement between members of staff about the purposes and value of assessment, and consequently what they feel they need to know.

Using such an activity will give you a list of skills, abilities, knowledge, personal characteristics, etc. which teachers will then need to find ways of assessing.

3   What kind of assessment?

This will, to a considerable extent, flow from the relative emphasis placed on the formative and summative aspects of assessment detailed above.

The assessment approach with which teachers are most familiar is **Norm-referenced** testing. This compares one student's performance with the 'norm' for the group. Thus a particular attainment, in say a GCSE paper or a spelling test, means nothing until held up against the scores of others taking the same exam. Teachers know well the shortcomings of this approach. Pupils do not know how to improve their performance as their scores depend entirely on their relative position within the class or group. A child may strive to do his/her very best in mathematics for ten years yet never feel that he or she has been successful nor improved his or her position. It is a guarantee of failure for most of our children as the majority can never be 'above average'.

Ipsative referencing compares a student's performance with the same student's earlier achievements. Thus improvement can be tracked accurately and children provided with a means to examine their own progress provided that each assessment is **Criterion referenced**.

As the name implies, this means that the task has defined criteria for success, about which pupils are informed and against which judgements are made.

The Schools Examination and Assessment Council (SEAC) believes that each assessment for each child should be based on evidence of that child's performance in relation to Statements of Attainment. Teachers must be able to say to any parent that each assessment was based on that child's work, rather than on a vague intuitive impression of the child's position in the class. This principle cannot be over-emphasised as it is much more likely to enable assessment to support diagnosis, planning and differentiation for both individual children and for the curriculum as a whole.

Assessment is important because at its heart is an understanding of children's learning. Learning is most effective when its purpose is clear to the learner. Your school policy also has a duty to interpret the curriculum to relate to the ways in which children learn, and to ensure that they are aware of the process they are in. Where possible children should be involved in the planning of their own learning. They should be clearly aware of the criteria on which assessment takes place. If children do not know why they are doing something, do not realise its relationship to what went before and what might follow, are not told what criteria are used to decide whether outcomes are good, bad or indifferent, how can they improve their performance? There are too many children in schools who, as far as their learning is concerned, are playing enormous guessing games. They should be brought in from the outside. We must do things **with** our children, not **to** them. With such messages at the heart of your discussions, you can exert a strong influence on every aspect of the curriculum.

4   Involve the whole staff.

As 'whole-school policy' implies, these assessment issues are for **all** teachers, not just those teaching Years 2 and 6 at the end of National Curriculum Key Stages when the statutory assessment process takes place. If you are to use this as a catalyst for improvement, then it is essential that all staff should be involved in drawing up policy and that it should be clear and agreed.

If you appoint a coordinator for assessment he or she will need to be seen as leader, enabler, researcher and resourcer but not a lone expert. It is essential to plan as a whole school, reaching professional consensus on the key issues.

5   Support the policy.

In addition, a successful policy will have to address the needs of staff for appropriate in-service education and training for assessment and to ensure that the resources and materials necessary to support the policy are available.

Once the broad philosophical approach to assessment has been established and agreed and the overall strategy identified, you need to get the detailed procedures and arrangements worked out and put into practice.

■ Curriculum planning and assessment

Assessment is an integral part of the curriculum and must be seen as one of the central planning issues. You need to be aware, at the planning stage, how teachers intend to enable each child to demonstrate fully and positively what he or she knows, understands and can do. Good planning will enable the school to use the curriculum to optimise children's learning and teachers' ability to assess that learning.

The approach to curriculum planning outlined here is not driven by a need to meet the demands or requirements of any particular curriculum, because a good process of planning is appropriate to any curriculum. Clearly though, it is necessary to demonstrate that the National Curriculum Attainment Targets, Statements of Attainment and Programmes of Study and the statutory assessment requirements are being met.

When we are planning the curriculum we need to keep this clearly in mind. What is the content to be? What processes will the children go through? What outcomes do we expect in terms of products? What earning outcomes do we expect in terms of the development of concepts, attitudes, skills and knowledge? What will the children know, understand and be able to do as a result of the curriculum activity? When you have some clarity of purpose in these areas, the esourcing and organisational issues become much clearer.

The various components of the planning process divide into two broad areas:

MACRO - concerned with the whole curriculum plan to ensure breadth and balance, to identify content and relevance, to ensure differentiation, progression and continuity in broad terms.

MICRO - concerned with the detail of how and what individuals and groups of children learn in terms of concepts, attitudes, skills and knowledge.

Much school planning in the primary school is based upon a topic or thematic approach to the curriculum, rightly seeing it as 'a seamless web'. Striving to give it meaning and purpose by recognising that knowledge and understanding are not compartmentalised or fragmented, this practice recognises also that children's minds are eclectic and not organised on subject lines.

A topic web is often used to explore all of the possibilities of a theme. It can be done in groups, using brainstorming techniques, collecting ideas under curriculum and cross-curricular headings and relating these to the requirements of the National Curriculum Statements of Attainment and Programmes of Study.

This process may be entirely satisfactory for the kind of MACRO planning identified above but when it goes no further it does not adequately detail the children's learning.

The following framework addresses this problem:

Planning a learning activity

1 **Context:** How does the activity relate to the whole curriculum policy?

2 **Aim:** What is the specific aim of the activity?

3 **Content:** What will the children be doing?

4 **Resources:** What resources will be required?

5 **Organisation:** How will the children be grouped?

What is the balance between different modes of learning and teaching style?

6 **Anticipated outcomes:** in terms of

- products;

- learning/developing concepts, attitudes, skills and knowledge.

7 **Assessment:** What criteria will be used and evidence looked for?

8 **Recording:** How will outcomes and processes be recorded?

9 **Evaluation:** To what extent were the stated aims and anticipated outcomes achieved? Why?

TRAINING DAY ACTIVITY FOR TWO TEACHERS
Planning

Think of a learning activity that you have used recently with a child or group and analyze it in terms of the planning model above. Reflecting upon an actual activity is better than using a hypothetical one.

Discuss this with another member of staff with children of a similar age.

Try out the other teacher's activity with your own class or group replanning according to the results of your discussion.

The model is a comprehensive one: the elements of outcomes assessment and recording are essential if the task of accurately assessing your children's attainments and achievements is to be possible. Planning is only the first stage in the assessment process. The plan has to be implemented and it will have to work.

▓ Classroom organisation and assessment

In considering the practicalities of implementing your curriculum lan, which will enable you to teach and assess your children ffectively and accurately, your first challenge is the busy nature of the 1odern classroom.

The assessment of children by teachers should draw on everyday aching activities: talking to children, listening to what they say, vatching them at work, drawing conclusions from what they do, oting the important things. A simple description of a complex set of tructures. But this does force us to focus on children, on the fact that hildren are in classrooms and teaching areas and that teachers 1emselves are best placed to assess their school achievements and ttainments accurately.

But in a class of 30 children, on average about three per cent of acher time is available per child. So how do the ways in which we perate in classrooms hinder or facilitate our success in assessing 1dividual children? What teacher behaviour, organisation and 1anagement skills will be necessary to ensure that the evidence and utcomes we have planned for are:

- elicited?

- noticed?

- understood?

This is the crux of the assessment task and takes us clearly and entrally into children learning and teachers teaching. It is essential that he time we have with children is good quality, effectively used time. 'his is necessary in order to acquire the information we need to teach nd assess and thus inform future planning to match activities to hildren's learning needs.

The professional challenge is therefore to find out about:

- what children know, understand and can do;

- the rate at which they learn;

- what they have learnt so far;

- what activities or experience should be provided or repeated;

- what their strengths and weaknesses are;

- the ways in which they learn best;

- what attitudes and opinions they have;

- what learning should take place next.

As a teacher, the professional challenge is also to find out about yourself:

- whether you have enough contact with each child;

- whether your teaching is effective;

- whether you are providing equal access to the curriculum for each child;

- whether you are making it easy for each child to learn;

- whether your resources and equipment are adequate;

- whether you are basing your decisions on assessments;

- whether your provision is suited to each child's developmental stage.

The challenge is to involve each child and motivate them all to achieve their learning potential.

Meeting this challenge will impel us to consider practical issues: of time management; of the management of space and physical resources; of the grouping of children; of the organisation and delivery of curriculum content.

▆ Time management

How can time be 'made'?

The management style of classrooms in the school may or may not promote the most efficient use of time. Here is a self-check list for you to put before your teachers and for them to consider:

- Does your classroom organisation allow you to teach, observe and listen to your children?

- Are the children encouraged to be independent? Does the classroom organisation support independence?

- Do all the children know what they are expected to do and why?

- Are the children encouraged to help each other and only refer to the teacher when necessary?

- Are the children encouraged to attempt things for themselves and are their attempts valued?

- Are there sufficient support materials available, for example, dictionaries and word banks, and are they sufficiently labelled/sign-posted?

- Do the children know what to do when they have completed a task?

- Are the resources clearly labelled and displayed to enable children to have easy access and to be able to use them independently?

- Do the children know when the teacher should not be interrupted?

- Are the children sometimes given responsibility for assessing/marking their own work which the teacher then monitors?

- Have you planned carefully enough for those children who will make heavy demands on your time?

- Are you aware of all things you do?

TRAINING DAY ACTIVITY FOR CLASS TEACHERS
Time management

Make a list of all the activities with which you are involved during the day, for example talking to children, marking, getting out resources, giving instructions. From this list identify those activities which:

a) enable you to teach or observe or assess. These are high-level activities, such as questioning and listening.

b) stop you from teaching or observing or assessing. These are low-level activities such as getting out equipment, supplying spellings.

Discuss with other staff how you can find more time for the high-level activities by reducing the low-level ones? Each teacher might have individual techniques of use to others to tackle these time-wasters.

All of those elements will be easier to achieve if the school has developed a policy for classroom management and organisation that develops continuity of expectation. This will ensure that children do not have to learn new rules and procedures for each teaching and learning area.

▆ Pupil grouping

Consideration of the suitability of the various group arrangements, used in classrooms for both learning and assessment, will assist teachers to understand the relative effectiveness of various alternatives.

If children are able to work together co-operatively the effective use of time and resources in a classroom will undoubtedly be strengthened. This will not happen automatically. 'Groups' are often merely seating arrangements where children still work as individuals. Teachers may need reminding that group tasks need to be designed specifically to encourage co-operative group work.

Types of groups will include one or more individuals working alone; one or more working in a small group; several children engaged in the same task; several children working co-operatively on a group activity; several children working in the same area; several children using a particular piece of equipment or apparatus.

Groups are frequently organised by age, interest, friendship, attainment in mathematics or reading, or at random...

The important issues, however, are the reasons and purposes for grouping, and the extent to which groupings enable the following to be achieved:

- To address the individual needs of children more easily;

- To make effective use of available resources;

- To involve all the children in discussion;

- To encourage the children to listen to and take account of each other's ideas and suggestions;

- To equalise opportunity of provision;

- To provide opportunities for assessment.

TRAINING DAY FOR CLASS TEACHERS

Pupil grouping

Some questions to consider individually and then to discuss in triads (groups of three).

Does your grouping of children reflect the overall aims of the school?

When was the last time you changed the groupings in your classroom? Why?

What criteria do you use for forming groups?

Are your groups formed according to the learning objectives?

Are your groups flexible?

Does the group structure reflect the nature of different tasks?

What strategies do you employ to give groups the opportunity to be responsible for their learning?

How do you ensure equal opportunity within each group?

The plenary should help you to clarify key points in the school's policy on the grouping of pupils.

■ Resources

The ability to ensure the time and space necessary to interact with individuals and groups of children for high-level activities which will facilitate successful teaching and assessment is also affected by resourcing issues. Time and energy are wasted, when resources are inadequate and disorganised. The maintenance and distribution of resources is one of the most fundamental of responsibilities of managers. Headteachers might from time to time examine the level of resources themselves, and determine what effect they could have on the improvement of standards in the school by using a checklist such as this:

1   Ask teachers to make a comprehensive list of all the materials which will be needed for their next class, year group, whole school topic or other learning activity:

   • books, reference materials, library loans;

   • artifacts, source materials;

   • TV, radio, video, tapes, computer programmes;

- materials, games, equipment tools;
- visits, visiting speakers.

How did you know about each of these items; does everyone on the staff have similar facilities?

2   Where will these items come from:

- the school: self, other teachers, central store;
- the home: child, parent;
- others: library, museum, voluntary organisation, local industry.

Are each of these areas fully exploited?

3   What changes will be needed to ensure that resources are accessible to the children and are organised effectively?

a) In the classroom:

- Are the materials stored near to where they will be used?
- Are they safe?
- Is storage labelled so that everyone will know the contents and be able to return them? Is this a learning experience itself?
- How are children involved in the care and management of equipment?
- Does the organisation of classroom resources encourage children to be independent, gather their own equipment, make decisions and have class ownership?

b) Centrally based resources:

- Is there a rationale for centrally-stored materials?
- Is there open access, if not who are the key holders? Why?
- Can children have access? Why?
- Which resources need secure storage?
- What system do you have for identifying where specific resources are at any given time?

- Are there appropriate labels for all central resources?

- How are AVA resources organised?

- What central materials for learning are available?

- How are staff and children made aware of these resources?

- Is there a catalogue of all school resources?
  How and by whom is it up-dated?

- Are subject-specific resources separately identified?

- Are children actively encouraged to participate in managing central resources?

- What strategies do you have for reviewing the availability and deployment of resources?

4   Are the resources suitable for the child?

Are they clean and inviting?

Are they at appropriate height level?

Are they matched to ability, develolpment, readability, age, interest?

Are they unbiased, unprejudiced, status free, supportive of equal opportunities, informed and accurate, concerned with real issues in society, global?

5   Are there any other people who can be helpful and do you involve them in your plans?

- peers, parents, classroom helpers, support personnel, governors, the wider community?

Assessment and pupil-teacher interaction

Conditions which enable teachers to make accurate judgements about children's attainment are identical to those needed for good teaching. Improvement in one will lead to improvement in the other.

Once the necessary time and space has been created for effective teaching, learning and the assessment of that learning it must be used effectively. As Headteacher you will want to be sure that teachers can listen to children effectively, recognise their learning and understand it.

Teachers as a group are talkers. They are not always so effective as listeners. Effective organisation for assessment will give children the time and the space to make clear their meanings, perceptions, understandings and knowledge. The skilled teacher must know when to prompt and when to intervene and when just to listen. Observation and listening, as children are given the opportunity to explore their learning freely in language, can be enormously revealing. Teachers must also gain an understanding of open and closed questions and their appropriateness to the context.

Improvement in this area of teaching requires honest self-analysis and clear self-knowledge. The really brave have used modern technology with tape recorders and video recorders to record and analyze their performance! But the use of videos of teachers at work in general can provide the basis of useful group discussion on this topic.

Where the whole staff in a school can co-operate openly and with constructive criticism in this area, not only is the ability to assess children enhanced, but so is the team quality of the school.

■ The collection and recording of evidence of attainment

The evidence of attainment must now be collected and recorded for assessment and reporting purposes. There are different kinds of evidence and a range of ways of collecting and recording it. These will include the following:

1 **Record and tick sheets** with boxes of various kinds based on the Attainment Targets, Statements of Attainment and Programmes of Study of the National Curriculum, as well as some reference to cross-curricular dimensions, skills and issues. They should be seen as both a teacher's and a school's record of work covered and are necessasry tools to keep track of the many parts of the primary school curriculum. Many schools have found it useful to incorporate symbols to indicate a teacher's judgement as to whether, for example, knowledge has been retained, a skill mastered, a concept understood.

2 The completion of such recording sheets may be aided by 'on the hoof' **note-taking**, and some schools are developing specific note pads for this purpose which incorporate shorthand symbols referring to the National Curriculum and to the level of learning.

Children may have to become accustomed to their teachers taking a few seconds to fill these in during a teaching activity.

3   Sometimes there will be no notes, no tick-boxes only the **teacher's knowledge and judgement** held in her head, which can be recounted orally based upon descriptions of children's behaviour. We must retain the confidence to trust the professional competence of teachers, in many areas.

4   Then there is the **portfolio of work outcomes**; pictures, stories, writing of all kinds, calculations, graphs, diagrams, models and perhaps even tape and video recordings, although we have to be realistic about the amount of evidence it is sensible to retain. The evidence can be annotated by the teacher, explaining its context and significance to the child's learning. Some schools have developed standard annotation pro-formas.

Teachers may need to be helped to prioritise so as to make the task at the end of the Key Stage more manageable.

The evidence collected must allow for:

- support of teacher's judgement;

- illumination of context and meaning to tick-box records;

- the sharing of standards. This has not proved to be an easy task but moderation of some kind is essential to agree about the meaning and interpretation of Statements of Attainment and whether an example of work fulfils them. A school's management of assessment must involve agreement and moderation meetings;

- importantly, the involvement of children, students and their parents in the process.

The portfolio of evidence could easily become unmanageable. Keep only that evidence which marks a significant step in a child's learning. Much evidence will become redundant as learning progresses, but you may want to keep the **first** pieces of evidence a child produces in order to make judgements about his or her long-term progress and show the 'value added' to the child's learning by the school. This is a fairer indication of a school's success than a comparison of the end assessment position, given the varying starting points and circumstances of individual children. Some schools and local education authorities have introduced 'base-line testing' to produce a statement of a child's starting point negotiated and agreed with parents.

■ Reporting to parents

Finally, the school has to decide how its assessment of children and the evidence of that assessment is to be reported to parents. The minimum statutory requirement is an annual written report on the subjects of the National Curriculum and other activities and Religious Education, accompanied in the end of Key Stage years by the core subject assessments at profile component and subject level.

A comprehensive pupil-profiling system will be essential if the assessment process is not to be reduced to a series of meaningless figures. This system celebrates the success of a child whatever the level of attainment and aims so as to give the child self-confidence, self-esteem and a sense of being, valued for what he or she is, at the same time as ensuring that his or her attainment in all areas of school life is accurately recorded.

At this point it will be useful to suggest that there is a distinction between a child's record of achievement and a comprehensive pupil profile. The record of achievement has at its heart a desire to celebrate the success of a child whatever the level of attainment. Its focus is self-confidence, self-esteem and valuing the child for what he or she is. Often children are confident themselves in choosing what should be in their record of achievement. This wholly admirable process however, does not necessarily fulfil the legal assessment requirements.

■ Managing SATs

The annual administration of Standard Assessment Tasks needs to be managed carefully to minimise the disruptive effect on normal teaching programmes, allocating the appropriate staffing and budgeting which is needed to support the process.

Headteachers need to show they can use the compulsory processes to improve their knowledge of the effectiveness of the teaching in their school and help teachers to organise their teaching to gain a more detailed understanding of children's learning needs. If this is the case then the efforts will have been worthwhile, the process stimulating, and the end result a strengthening of the profession.

9 Marketing the primary school

Why promote your school?

Every Primary School has an image and a reputation to uphold. It is because we have paid insufficient attention to this matter that state schools in Britain have had a very poor public image. Indeed, since the mid 1970s the education service has scored, what Michael Brunt in *Marketing Schools* refers to as, several own goals. He includes the William Tyndale affair, the Great Debate, the disruption caused by pay disputes and the Ray Honeyford Saga. This has left the impression in the public's mind that schools are inadequately equipped, understaffed by incompetent teachers who fail to teach indisciplined children to read and write. It is no wonder that members of the public frequently express general dissatisfaction with state education.

This contrasts, however, with our everyday experience of talking to parents, who seem to be reasonably satisfied with the school which their own children attend. This implies that the more parents know about a particular institution the happier they are with it. It is usually 'other schools' with which they associate the general media message which is less than flattering.

It is not therefore merely a question of whether individuals are right or wrong, but a question of what people believe or can be persuaded to believe that is important. As a leader of your school, you need to understand that such beliefs can be and are manipulated, controlled and changed.

Celebrate the 'Good News'

The first line of defence is to attack and to fight with the best weapons to hand, the excellent work going on in your own school. Each school needs to be active in spreading the good news about its everyday creative, interesting, exciting and successful achievements.

Parents, governors and other community members need to be fully informed about the many good things which are happening in order to sell education to a sceptical audience.

You need to project your school in an image-conscious society. The lack of image promotion may say as much about your school as any rumours that go around the estate.

You need to encourage and gain the support of parents, governors and the members of the community in your promotional activities. Fund-raising activities help a school to develop in both a social and material sense and project an identity. Deliberately setting out to use the positive features of the school to further develop these activities is a natural progression.

■ The rationale behind image promotion

a) **Raising staff morale**

Many Headteachers consider putting the school image forward as a way of raising the morale of all staff and others involved in school. Staff like to be part of a school which is held in high regard by the local community.

b) **More open enrolment**

It is more important than ever for schools to maintain and increase their enrolment. Parental choice of school has increased its importance, and as under formula funding, extra resource is made available to the governors for every child the school attracts.

c) **Community links**

Marketing the Primary School has also become popular recently because of the importance of community and industry. The widening educational partnership through the Governing Body has produced opportunities to generate extra income and resources from the business community. The benefits of sponsorship and cooperation with industry may help extend the entire school curriculum and improve its delivery. Money will come to what is perceived as a successful, effective school.

d) **Success breeds success**

Successful schools of which parents and children are proud of, tend to generate success in a self-fulfilling prophecy. They have a successful educational effect upon the children. Parents trust the staff and reinforce what teachers tell the children; the children benefit from being seen by friends and neighbours as successful products of the educational system and grow to believe in their own capabilities. A recipe for success. Public relations and marketing therefore play an important role in helping children make the most of their educational opportunities.

What is marketing?

In their book *Marketing the School*, Michael Marland and Rick Rogers emphasise that 'There is no technique required by marketing that is not used in some aspect or other of the teaching tasks already undertaken by the school, and there is no mystique about marketing skills.' However, the image of the marketing man who would sell his own grandmother for profit is one which lingers, and one to which schools rightly do not wish to subscribe. Geoff Bowles in *Marketing and Promotion* warns that some Headteachers will be faced with negative attitudes because 'confusion arises where marketing is equated with selling, which is seen as the unscrupulous manipulation of the customer in an attempt to foist a scond-rate product on her (or him) or thought of as window-dressing in an attempt to hide the shallowness of the rest of the enterprise'. He goes on to argue that marketing professionals would regard both of these activities as unproductive even in the short term. However, this is the impression many teachers have of the activity.

It is therefore important to be clear about what is meant by 'Marketing the School'. Marketing is simply the process of satisfying customer needs efficiently. It has also been described as everything to do with focusing on client needs and their satisfaction. Thus schools with the primary object of deserving, acquiring and retaining a good reputation are engaged in a process of marketing. If you can focus on what your different clients and customers require of your institution, you may respond to the outside world slightly differently. The result at first, might simply be in the responses your staff make to requests from parents, the manner in which they answer the telephone or the style of notes sent home to parents. You might begin to set up planned and rational structures in your school, to help communicate your preferred image and enhanced reputation to your clients and your customers. Make no mistake: if you fail to cultivate an image for yourself then this will be done for you in ways which are outside your control. It is no accident that hard-headed banks, councils and soap-powder manufacturers spend so much on establishing an identity and promoting their image. They do it 'because it works'.

◼ First moves in marketing

Identify your client

Who are our clients? In the primary school most of us would accept that parents of the pupils are the clients as they are in law (as Macbeth reminds us clearly in his book *Involving Parents*) and that the teachers are therefore responsible or accountable to them. But the local community may also be viewed as a client. The funding of schools via the business rates and local taxation are a measure of this. For young children the parent will be the one who makes the choice of school. Parents and children influence each other in this matter of choice. A child coming home and discussing good or bad experiences at school with parents will influence parental opinion. Parents and children may be the immediate customers but they will be influenced by a broader group of clients, like local employers, local businessmen and the local community. This group will therefore be significant in marketing terms. The opinions of teachers in the secondary or middle schools to which your children transfer, those who work with the Cubs and Brownie packs, leaders in the local mosque, are all likely to have an effect on the standing of your school in the community.

While building up a clear picture of who your customers are, you will need to ensure that everything you are offering is right for as many children as possible.

A marketing audit

Before you embark on the promotional activities that you have planned, you need to ask yourself, 'What are people saying about my school?' You will need to ask questions about your image and standing, how you are currently perceived by your customers, potential customers and opinion formers in the community. '*There are various avenues of information ranging from the school gate parliament, local Rotary club, PTA, non-teaching staff and local shopkeepers.*' As Geoff Bowles describes, '*None has a monopoly on the truth and it will be necessary to interpret the information for its degree of partiality, optimism and pessimism*'.

You will have to carry out some research both within the school and externally by eliciting the wishes and concerns of parents. The audit will provide information about:

A   CURRICULUM DEVELOPMENT

- If we compare our business to that of an industrial or

commercial concern then it is our curriculum which is on offer.

- The educational equivalent to product development is curriculum development. Are there weaknesses in this area which need attention?

- How do the Governors, the non-teaching staff and the influential parents see the curriculum role of your school?

- Your attitude to this idea will be revealing. In many schools this area remains the 'no parents past this point' zone of yesteryear.

B   TIMETABLING AND ORGANISATION

- Have you got the balance right, do parents feel, that there is too much of one thing and not enough of another? Are there extra-curricular activities parents would like to see?

- How do parents regard the timing of the children's day, the grouping arrangements within classes, the vertical grouping of classes?

- How do the professionals feel about justifying their decisions to parents on these matters?

Your public relations audit will need to consist of both an external and internal audit.

The external audit

What do you know about the school's image? You must consider how others in the community perceive your school:

- Ask feeder schools and playgroup leaders about your image with parents of young children in the district.

- Enlist the help of parents, governors or local businessmen who live locally and who are already involved with your school.

- Invite and welcome comments from ex-pupils and their parents.

- Measure your standing in the local community alongside other schools.

- Ask parents or children who choose your school after visiting others why they did so.

Are you willing to make changes in your school to keep up with your competitors? The degree to which you may wish to pursue opinions on your school, according to Michael Brunt in *Marketing Schools*, will depend upon whether you view criticism as an evil to be survived or a useful source of information which may help you to improve working practices and customer relations. Which applies to you? There are two effective ways of finding out clients' opinions.

A questionnaire

1 It is more likely that respondents will answer yes/no questions than construct written answers. Yes/no answers are also easier to analyze.

2 The answers may be more honest if the questionnaire is anonymous.

3 Accentuate the positive qualities of the school in the questionnaire.

4 Make the completed forms the entry for a raffle or give some other sort of incentive to maximise the number of questionnaires returned.

A specimen questionnaire will be found in Appendix A. This was used with a variety of schools to find out the opinion of parents whose children had recently entered their school. Why had they chosen this school? What impressed them? What was the general feeling about the school in the community? It was presented to the parents as a pilot study. In this way, parents were made to feel that in joining in with this exercise they would be giving information both of immediate use and would also be contributing to a wider knowledge of why parents choose certain schools and this school in particular.

A discussion group

Discussion groups are useful for generating ideas or for going into issues in more detail. Ideally, you need to form groups of seven or eight parents. A balanced group is very important here because you need a broad and balanced view of the school's perceived strengths and weaknesses, not just the views of the vociferous minority.

A starting point for the discussion might be comments on the results of the questionnaire. Many schools have been quite successful in this kind of activity by themselves, but others have commissioned surveys in conjunction with university and polytechnic departments of education. Responses are more likely to be valid if the group leader is not someone with a vested interest in the school. In either case one thing has been proved. You are showing your community that you are interested in and are actively measuring the perception of the school within that community. The impact of any policy may be small, but if you are seen to be interested in improvement this may be more influential than the policy changes themselves.

The internal audit

The second stage in your assessment of public reputation is the internal audit. This is an examination of your school's Strengths, Weaknesses, Opportunities and Threats (SWOT for short). This needs to be applied to every aspect of school life and work and should ideally involve all staff, teaching, ancillary, secretarial, caretaking, cleaning.

An internal audit will seek to assess the strengths and weaknesses of the school itself and the opportunities and threats offered by its environment. A number of suggested strategies to enable you to secure this information can be found in Kotler and Fox's book *Strategic Marketing for Educational Institutions* published in 1985.

A **SWOT** analysis checklist might consist of:

Strengths
The things your school is good at.
Good academic achievement, good community links, strong inter-school liaison, committed teachers, good resources and facilities, etc.

Weaknesses
The things which let your school down and hold it back.
Weak staff members or poor facilities, poor use of equipment, behaviour of the children on the way home, rubbish dumped on the spare land beside the school.

Opportunities
Your school's potential for the future.
New educational opportunities you can foresee, housing development projects in the locality, new ideas, new appointments.

Threats
The potential problems your school faces.
Loss of pupils, loss of key staff, local unemployment, competition from neighbouring schools.

Identify two or three specific points in each of the SWOT categories – more than this will confuse the issue. When you have completed the analyses of the survey you should have a clearer picture of your strengths in depth and have started to identify areas in need of attention.

■ Solutions – your unique selling position

It should now be possible to feed the information from both stages of the public relations audit back to the clients, i.e. the parents and pupils. This will help to identify targets for the school's marketing plan and if possible to identify the Unique Selling Position (USP). There must be one particular thing or blend of things that your school can offer which makes it different from its competitors and which you can highlight in your promotions.

There need be no such thing as the one best school in the district, just as there is no one best car or toothpaste. Marketeers know that a single scale of excellence is an advantage only to the one at the top of that scale. One company will manufacture a variety of soap powders, but advertise a different quality for each brand to appeal to different customers: a better smell, softer rinse, better for automatic machines, kinder to clothes, cheaper per wash. Product diversity is the key. In *Creating an Excellent School* by H. Beare (et al) the authors argue that if schools act in a similar way and many educational scales of excellence can be created, then there will be a place in the sun for many schools.

It is not a difficult task. In 'Image-makers of the Sixth', Ian Nash writes that one recent survey of secondary school Headteachers and governors showed that they had little difficulty identifying their own USPs.

Thus you must ask:

- What makes my school unique in its lessons, policies, staff results or facilities?

- What characterises education here as opposed to other schools?

- What trade mark do members of this school carry with them after they leave?

If the answer is none, then your first course of action is clear, do something about it or resign!

■ The marketing plan

Having surveyed clients' satisfaction with your school and analyzed strengths and weaknesses, your next stage in the marketing cycle is the development of a plan involving strategies and objectives which need to be achieved. This should be based on the data collected from your information gathering phase. It should not be a bolt-on adjunct to other school development plans but will be an integral part of the whole-school development, and as such it should be concerned with both short-term and long-term objectives. You must also ensure that the implementation schedule is clearly defined, resources earmarked, and an assessment of monitoring functions built into the overall plan. It is also essential at this stage, that you gain whole-staff commitment to these marketing objectives. If you are not going to tackle the responsibility of marketing the school yourself, you need to appoint someone from your staff who will be able to take on the job. Many primary schools are new to marketing and making such appointments is a novel feature, sometimes tied to an incentive allowance. Other schools have been successful in giving this responsibility to a group of interested teachers who form themselves into a marketing committee.

■ Applying effective marketing theory

When preparing your marketing plan for the school, nothing else should be decided in terms of its planned strategy for success, until the marketing 'mission' has been finalised and agreed. The children's interests must come first. The decisions concerning the ways in which these interests will be fulfilled will then follow naturally. Next will come the tactical issues concerning the role of marketing the school. Having built up a clear picture through internal and external market research as to who the target group is, your school will need to ensure that everything you are offering will be right for as many children and parents as possible.

■ The marketing mix

This leads us into a consideration of the marketing mix of the four Ps namely Product, Place, Price and Promotion. The marketing mix is a set of controlled variants which you can use in order to implement the agreed school marketing strategy – in a way that will accomplish the mission, statement and objectives as defined in the school marketing plan.

▓ Product

The 'product' which you are offering is your curriculum and its delivery; its range and options; how it leads to other stages and the extra-curricular activities available to the children.

You need to be clear about:

- what your school does for its customers;
- the costs to the customers in terms of time, effort, not choosing another shool, etc.
- what special features you can offer your customers.

▓ Place

The next dimension of the marketing mix is that of place – the physical environment of your school. Many schools, even the most prestigious, have some buildings or equipment which are in evident need of refurbishment. There may well be good reasons for this but prospective parent customers do not come to visit your school to hear about your problems! At a minimum you have to be sure that those parts of the school which they do see look clean, tidy and well cared for. The school foyer or entrance area is a crucial place as it is the first part of the school which visiting parents will see. It should go without saying that it needs to look as inviting and welcoming as possible, particularly if it will be used as a waiting area.

- Is the school easy to find?
- Do you have prepared an up-to-date map directing visitors to the school from all major points?
- Is it clear where visitors may park?
- Are there signs to the office entrance/reception?

Some of the best are designed and made by children using clip-art and wordprocessing packages on the computer.

- Is there a display of work and achievement for visitors to look at? Are school press-cuttings on a board or in a scrap book?

- Are visitors to the school warmly received?

- Do staff answer the telephone considerately?

> **Remember first impressions are the most important!**

■ Price

For schools in the state sector, the cash to run the school is very much tied up with formula funding. Apart from this income, Parent Teacher Associations, sponsorship and school lettings may generate additional revenue. Parents are often impressed with just what can be done on a limited budget. Value for money is associated with a good buy.

Additional funding will, of course, make the job of effective image promotion easier. Sponsorship is a valuable source of such revenue.

There are many kinds of sponsorship you may wish to consider. Some of the following ways have been used to attract additional revenue or make monies stretch further:

- grants from charitable trusts;

- gifts of prizes and trophies;

- the free use of equipment and other facilities;

- discounted goods;

- support through promotional activities;

- sale of school produce;

- advertisements in school brochures and magazines;

- fund raising and other charitable contributions, including parents' covenants.

To attract sponsorship for your school, your approach needs to be systematically thought through.

You need to do the following:

1 Research your selected sponsors properly to discover whether they have given any help in the past and which activities they have supported – also to check on whether they are already supporting other schools in the locality.

2 Send a letter of application to a named person wherever

possible, outlining your request in clear terms, keeping your letter brief and to the point.

3 Ask for sponsorship for a specific item or programme, which could be presented or opened at a ceremony. This is much more effective than asking for a contribution to, what might appear to be, a vague fund.

4 Be clear about the potential benefits to the sponsoring body. Will they get free advertising to parents? Will the community associate them with quality and respectability because of their relationship with you? Are your parents a large potential market for their goods or services? Are they a large local employer concerned about their image in the community?

5 Follow up your application – a negative response does not mean that all is lost – you may have to join the queue or wait until the next round of sponsorship funding.

You may wish to seek guidance from the governors in order to defray any criticism and cut out the potential embarrassment of awards from inappropriate bodies (tobacco and drinks companies, for example).

You may wish to:

- open your building for renting after school hours and during school holidays. (Be careful to check all the legal and insurance implications of doing this.)

- offer the use of your school grounds for fetes, garden parties, caravan club weekends, etc.

- invite local organisations to consider using your school premises for their meetings from time to time.

Do, however, take note of the interests of local residents who may not welcome car-parking problems and a repetitive 'Morris Dancing' tape being played all day across the school field on their day of rest!

Promotion

The final variable in the marketing mix is that of promotion – your public relations campaign.

This is designed to communicate your good reputation and develop the mutual understanding, which is so important between you and your client/potential clients and community.

PR activities could include some, or all, of the following:

- brochures;

- press releases;

- newsletters;

- open days;

- competitions;

- articles;

- meetings/discussions.

Schools have extensive experience of organising events. Many PR opportunities are presented by the Christmas Concert, PTA Summer Fayre, a school trip to somewhere unusual, Sports Day or a special visitor.

Strategies for school promotion need to be considered at the event-planning stage. The event can be a window to parents and the community, which gives the school an opportunity to create and present the right kind of image.

Public relations covers all kinds of communication with the public apart from direct advertising i.e. managing your communication with the client community.

The school brochure

The school brochure is probably the single most important piece of promotional literature that you are likely to produce. Compile your brochure having fully identified the image that you want for the school, and make sure it reflects that image.

- It must be an honest reflection of what is actually going on in the school.

- Consider format and size, A4 or A5. Presentation is most important. It needs to have the most attractive and practical format and size for the content you want to include.

- Use short paragraphs wherever possible and use 'white space' – you do not need to fill the page. Fill the covers and text of the brochure with plenty of illustrations or well-reproduced photos. Make sure that you use those which show children (both boys and girls) involved in school activities.

The contents should include the following:

1   A description of the benefits provided by the school.
2   A description of what the pupils will learn, perhaps written in question and answer format and certainly avoiding educational jargon.
3   A statement of your teaching and learning methods.
4   An indication of later progression available (if appropriate).
5   School credentials, with qualifications and experience of staff.
6   Contact name and telephone number of Headteacher.
7   Map of school and surrounding areas.

Make the information clear and include a list of the contents. Keep the brochure topical and avoid using information that will quickly date, e.g. the price of school uniform. Finally, think about whether you can defray some of the printing costs by attracting sponsorship for your brochure or by covering some or all of the costs through the inclusion of advertisements.

If your school does not have access to a Desk Top Publishing (DTP) package, which will manage the layout of both text and graphics, remember DTP also stands for 'Dab with Tippex and Photocopy'. A most professional result can be achieved by cutting and pasting items to white sheets, and after photocopying, producing a master by covering the edge shadows with Tippex. You could then have stiff front covers produced commercially (printed with school name and emblems/pictures/children's work). Use similar card for the back cover and bind with a plastic edge binder. This format is easy to update each year by substituting individual pages.

Making use of the media

The press, particularly the local press, is always glad to receive material from schools particularly if it is presented in an appropriate form and accompanied by pictures or illustrations. You need to encourage in your school a policy for a positive relationship with the press and ensure that staff are always on the look out for good news stories. Additionally you may find it useful to introduce yourself to and maintain contact with local newspaper correspondents and that all dealings between your school and the press go through your appointed press offices/marketing officer/media liaison officer, etc.

PREPARING A PRESS RELEASE

When writing a press release the following points should be taken into consideration. You need the following:

- A good headline which will attract imemdiate attention;

- A people/child centred angle;

- A list paragraph: Who

    What

    Why

    When

    Where

- Quotatable quotes (if appropriate) from a named individual;

- A photograph to back up the story;

- A contact name and telephone number.

Adapted from Brunt M. (1987) Marketing Schools

Other forms of the media which you could use are local TV, which might be interested if they could get an angle on a story which appealed to them, and radio, particularly if the radio station is community based. In their book *Marketing the School*, Michael Marland and Rick Rogers give some excellent guidance from the perspectives of both Headteacher and journalist to Headteachers dealing with the media (particularly if you are unfortunate enough to find yourself in a crisis situation).

■ Monitoring the marketing process (after-sales service)

Having established your mission and objectives, devised strategies for implementation, appointed an individual or committee with responsibility for marketing and set appropriate timescales, you need to build into your plan a monitoring and evaluation element to assess how effective your strategies have been. You could do this by informal discussion with parents or members of the local community or by surveying by questionnaire to past pupils and parents. An example of this is provided in C.Thompson's *Monitoring Client Satisfaction in Schools*, published in 1985.

■ Conclusion

When marketing, be positive, welcoming, show interest in everyone who calls for information, aim to build up trust and mutual understanding and, if possible, go out of your way to find acceptable alternatives. Michael Brunt reminds us '*Black and Decker...made its fortune not because potential customers wanted 8 mm drills but because they wanted the wherewithal to drill 8 mm holes*'. If we can identify parental wants, interpret them in the context of our own school and then turn those wants into needs, not only will our individual children benefit but so will the education service as a whole.

10 Managing the curriculum for quality

Your school will be judged by the changes it brings about in its pupils over time. These may be viewed in terms of attitudes, behaviour, respect for elders and property, but mostly by the knowledge and learning children have gained through being in your school. 'The management of the curriculum', state Alan and Audrey Paisley in their book *Effective Management in Primary Schools*, 'may be regarded as being almost identical with the management of the school itself' ... 'The curriculum remains the centrepiece of school life and its management ... the main preoccupation of the staff'. Certainly most things are judged as being crucial or peripheral to school life by their level of importance to this aspect of the school, and almost the entire productive capacity of the school is geared to this feature. Indeed the quality of our curriculum is our selling point (Chapter 9), the focus of our planning (Chapter 1), the purpose of staffing (Chapter 2), the motivation behind the appraisal process (Chapter 5), and will act as an appropriate indicator of the effectiveness of our spending policies (Chapter 7).

■ The management task

The central task facing Primary Headteachers and their senior colleagues is the management of the whole curriculum. The core and foundation subjects define very closely our curriculum content. This content has been enlarged upon by the provision of Programmes of Study and non-statutory guidance which accompany the subject curricula.

There is, however, no legal basis for the methods by which children are taught or the ways in which curriculum content is organised. It is this organisation and curriculum dissemination which becomes the area for decision making.

It is also true that the national curriculum is not the whole curriculum. Primary school leaders must take account of this fact. The

Education Reform Act requires schools to consider the curriculum as a whole, to ensure that it meets the requirement for a balanced and broadly-based curriculum as well as the delivery of the Programmes of Study.

The Local Education Authority will have established its own curriculum policy as required by Section 17 of the *Education Reform Act of 1986*. The governors are required to 'consider' this policy, and to resolve whether to modify it. The governors have full power to modify it, provided that they do not do this so extensively so that the original, is not recognised. Clearly, the management of the planning of the school's curriculum depends on this consideration, for legally the remainder of the school's curriculum planning will derive from the extent to which the governors, on behalf of the school, accept or modify the LEA's policy. Thus, considering the LEA's curriculum policy in the light of the school's aims and its own curriculum audit is an important step.

■ What is the whole curriculum?

When we consider what the implications of the 'whole' might be for curriculum management, we can identify a number of dimensions.

1 Time-span

Here Headteachers will need to consider the time-frame within which we should judge the breadth and balance of our work, the progression of concepts and the relative development of individuals. Are we looking for balance in one week/over a term/throughout a year? Is this suitable for all children or need it be staged differently for some?

2 Coverage

Headteachers and their staff must decide at what point in the term or week teachers offer various aspects of content to groups and individuals.

3 Process

These decisions concern the appropriate teaching, learning and assessment methods which pupils need to experience across content areas and over time.

Managing the whole curriculum means working for coherence as well as for breadth. It must also mean devising practical strategies to ensure that all pupils get access to their entitlement and that access embraces continuity and progression over time.

Figure 1 represents a model of the whole curriculum. Theoretically this model could apply to any period of time and any number of learners and be achieved by any given methodology. If this then is the whole curriculum to be managed, how is it to be done?

Figure 1   Each area of the curriculum may be examined as an issue of appropriate *timing*.

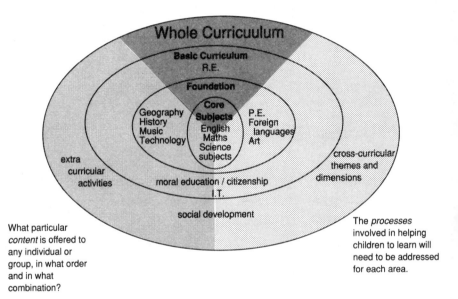

What particular *content* is offered to any individual or group, in what order and in what combination?

The *processes* involved in helping children to learn will need to be addressed for each area.

▪ How is the curriculum to be organised?

Since the second world war British primary education has built a strong tradition of how the curriculum should be organised and by which methods it should be taught. The progressive tradition of primary education was perhaps most clearly stated in the Plowden Report.

The basic premise of primary education has remained since that time, that the child is at the centre of our concerns, issues, teaching philosophy and *raison d'être*.

No-one needs to apologise for promoting a 'child-centred' approach, for if serving the interests of children is not the foremost mission that a primary school can have, then we ourselves serve no purpose.

However the term 'child-centred' has acquired pejorative overtones, and primary schools need to develop descriptions of their philosophies which show how the supportive and enabling tradition fulfils the current demands of society and the exploding expectations of parents.

For example we could describe:

A learner-focused curriculum:

- recognises the needs of society, the expectations of parents and the individual characteristics of children as learners;

- attempts to meet these needs through a differentiated approach to learning;

- is based upon what we know of the value of focused experiential learning, guided discovery and investigation;

- recognises that the interests of children can provide motivation for learning;

- attempts to take account of the effect of cultural background of children on their learning styles;

- is concerned with the devlopment of curiosity, perseverance and cooperation;

- understands that self-confidence, self-esteem and self-discipline underpin all learning.

A learner-focused philosophy directing the school's curriculum will give it shape and continuity. Principles such as these can be applied throughout all the facets of the school. Such a stance will pull together the strengths of the progressive primary tradition and the imperatives of centrally directed Programmes of Study.

It is only when the activities in a primary school are underpinned by a clearly thought-out, coherent, and agreed philosophical base that the eductional process will be successful. Practice which exists in a vacuum is ad-hoc, day-to-day, unguided by any general theory or direction will not be satisfactory. A major function of curriculum management is to ensure that this clear and agreed philosophy is established.

The philosophy must be broadly agreed in the school's aims and refined through more specific curricular objectives. Ultimately the philosophy must be realised in children's growth and learning.

Traditionally schools have used subject areas and their boundaries to

TRAINING DAY FOR CLASS TEACHERS

Learner-focused education

Divide teachers into groups and take a variety of statements from the list defining 'learner-focused education'. Use a different selection for each group and ask teachers to rank order the statements in order of importance, firstly to them personally and after discussion with their group.

If any differences emerge between teachers or between groups, use this as a focus for discussion.

Use the first ranked statements from each group as an example and by the same method ask each group to come up with some curricular objectives to realise the aims they have highlighted.

define their curricula. The National Curriculum carries this further so that common examples and experiences are children's entitlement.

Within these subject boundaries there exists a great deal of important knowledge which can contribute to a child's understanding of the world in which he or she lives and learns.

Subject boundaries can act as a straight-jacket, however, if we view knowledge and study skills from the perspective of the child's acquisition of concepts. For example, if we want to introduce children to the ideas of continuity and change, we could look at change of state in physical science (melting and boiling), growing older in biological science, in history (change of fashion) and geological change over a longer period. It seems that it is possible to tackle this area from a number of different stances, indeed we might argue that if we choose only one then the concept will be only partially established.

Similarly, a proper study of any subject involves the use of language. If isolated in an English lesson, language tends to become divorced from the occasion of its use 'for real'. Language is a crucial unifying factor in the curriculum. Mathematics in real life will not occur unless built into a curriculum model, where integrated skills are the main feature.

Once the idea of clearly defined and finite 'bodies of knowledge' seemed increasingly difficult to sustain, so curricula based upon them became suspect.

As a consequence most primary schools have continued to use a topic, theme or project approach to deliver the National Curriculum and beyond.

The aims of topic work include the following:

- To give children the opportunity to learn, develop and use a range of skills in the study of something they are aware of in their lives;

- To widen their knowledge and experience of the topic itself and through its study to make conceptual generalisations;

- To give children the experience of learning in different ways, from a variety of sources and through different media;

- Within their capabilities, to give children some opportunity to study on their own, to work independently, purposefully and with self-discipline in organising themselves in group and individual tasks and for some, to formulate their own ideas as to what their next steps might be;

- To give a degree of relevance to children's work and to establish the idea that study skills are for a purpose and not just an endless series of 'dummy runs'.

TRAINING DAY ACTIVITY

Topic work in the National Curriculum

Organise year-groups of teachers to attempt to match the claimed features of a topic approach with the curriculum objectives they formulated in response to the previous task. Can they also be matched with National Curriculum Attainment Targets (for example AT1 in mathematics and science, speaking and listening in English)?

Such an approach clearly fits into a learner-focused philosolphy. The prime curriculum management challenge of primary education is to match it with the closely defined content of knowledge and skills in the National Curriculum?

However subject matter is organised there remain important relationships between all areas of knowledge and those important skills and understandings – observation, calculation, communication, prediction, classification and so on, are relevant to all subject areas.

Perhaps there is an unnecessary tension between the learner-focused approach, taking children 'where they are' and the existence of a body of knowledge, no matter how dynamic and changing that body of knowledge is. We need to relate these in some way, they are not inimical. Perhaps it comes down to attitudes and careful planning.

If we believe with Arthur Razzel that the 'basics' in primary education remain as they have always been:

> finding out
> sorting out
> and recording

then we now just have a new context in which these skills can be developed.

The only practical way to be sure that the prescribed content is covered and that children's learning experiences are worthwhile is to plan collectively together in year groups or Key Stages to work out learning experiences for their pupils over time.

Managing curriculum planning

- Review existing resources to determine their best use.
- Scrutinise National Curriculum documents to identify overlaps in content and skills.
- Acknowledge that a cross-curricular approach is required to ensure balance, breadth and relevance.
- Abandon all-embracing, half-termly topics with their vague virtually unplanned content.
- Develop topics as interrelated teaching activities, delivering agreed and planned elements of the National Curriculum within a whole-school framework.

Planning is the key. The topic areas chosen will have to be clearly linked to the required outcomes, not conceived as an open-ended journey that has no destination, although open-ended learning activities will naturally be part of the methodology.

■ Managing curriculum time

Time allocated to such competing themes is of vital importance to achieve balance. A learner-focused curriculum would demand that time allocation takes account of what 'every learner brings (to the classroom, by way of) prior knowledge, skills and attitudes, so what appears to be a commonn curriculum for all is actually a different curriculum for each'. In his book *Managing School Time*, Brian Knight goes on to contrast models based on time input with time for specified outcomes.

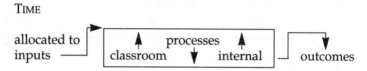

Here time is allocated to the priorities of the inputs: reading a long or a short story, doing two pages of Peak Maths, devising a fair test in science will be moderated by the classroom processes involved (some things take longer than others to do, resources are finite etc.).

An alternative model centres on the time required to achieve outcomes.

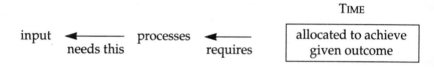

Our view of curriculum time alters with such a perspective. Thought of in this way, mathematics in Term 3 may be vastly different from the time priority given in Term 1. Certain children will need much longer in some subject areas than others to achieve the same outcome and in some topics within subjects.

In *A view from a primary school*, David Winkley debates the time implications of the subject versus integrated curriculum. He presents a number of models relating subject components to a class topic worth considering by Headteachers currently tackling this issue.

It needs flexibility and care in planning to deliver the vast and varied National Curriculum.

▓ Indicators of effectiveness

The success or otherwise of the curriculum you produce will be the main indicator of your effectiveness as a Headteacher. You can develop your own range of performance indicators as criteria for successful performance. The selection of statements will be crucial to the judgements made about the school and all staff should be involved.

TRAINING DAY ACTIVITY
Creating indicators of effectiveness

Get the senior management team to look at the lists of indicators reproduced below and construct two sets.

1 Those which are, and will continue to be, successfully achieved by the school.
2 Desirable achievements, on which judgements about schools to which they would like to send their own children may be made.

The trick is to match 1 and 2.

You need to decide on a limited number of key pieces of information. Share with your governors the reasons for your choices showing how you can help with monitoring and planning. Remember indicators are not ends in themselves; they have to be interpreted much in the same way that a doctor collects pulse rates, pallor and temperature. None is meaningful in itself, but each may indicate either singly, or taken together, that further investigation is necessary. Professional judgement will be exercised on this information. What measures will be helpful to the primary school management team?

Indicators of curricular achievements of pupils

- Age-range moderated teacher assessments of National Curriculum levels of attainment;
- Reading ages or other standardised scores;
- Progress made by individuals in the above;
- Important learning objectives or priorities achieved;
- Individual and team sporting successes.

Indicators of curriculum development activity

- Number, type and effectiveness of INSET courses attended;
- Further qualifications gained after initial training;
- Suitability of processes established to identify INSET needs;
- Arrangements for the induction of new staff and supply staff to ensure continuity of teaching;
- Use and variety of non-pupil contact days and their resultant impact in classrooms;
- Use of LEA curriculum support staff and impact on the curriculum;
- Invitations to staff of the school to contribute to LEA/inter school INSET;
- Established cycle of review of curricular areas.

Indicators of curricular provision

- Proven access to a broad, balanced, relevant and differentiated curriculum irrespective of race, gender and special needs;
- Worthwhile extensions to classroom work reflecting the interests of staff and pupils (clubs, holidays, day visits, external speakers);
- Size of teaching groups;
- Evidence of collaborative planning;
- Cleanliness of school, suitability of classroom furniture and equipment, displays, environment;
- Details of hardware and software available to support the curriculum;
- Evidence of the use of the results of teacher assessment to inform future planning;
- Diversity of teaching methods and matching of work to children's needs.

Indicators of parental satisfaction

- Size of waiting-list for admission;
- Number of out-of-district children;
- Attendance at annual governors' meeting, parents' evenings to report on children's progress and PTA events;

- Level and nature of complaints, withdrawals and compliments;

Indicators of curriculum managerial health

- Evidence that the needs of the whole school are reflected in the management system;

- Existence of an agreed mission statement which underpins all other policies;

- Permeation of corporate aims and objectives through: policy documents, school brochure, reporting activities, work in classrooms, resource allocation, distribution of incentive allowances;

- Participation of teachers, governors, parents and pupils in school-development planning;

- Arrangements to encourage consistency between agreed expectations and teacher performance;

- Arrangements to ensure continuity at rites of passage through the school;

- Evidence of an effective formal communication system throughout the school;

- Arrangements established for monitoring and evaluating the curricular consequences of spending decisions;

- Arrangements made for the monitoring of the effectiveness of teaching and learning in every classroom.

■ Conclusion

The Government School Management Task Force open their report by emphasising '*Successful schools do not simply happen: they are successful because people make them so and all such people have a stake in management*'. This chapter has brought together various strands of the prime management task facing primary Headteachers and their colleagues. That task is to produce a successful school curriculum, which will stand up to scrutiny. This will be done by working through others on the staff and agreeing the philosophical basis for the changes they want to make. Performance indicators will provide management information for the purposes of monitoring the development of the school's heart – its curriculum.

Appendix

University of Manchester
School of Education

Parental Choice
of Primary School

A pilot study into the factors which parents take into account when choosing a primary school for their children.

Mike Harrison
Lecturer in Education
Centre for Primary Education

Marie Brown
Lecturer in Management
& Marketing of Education

Question 1:   How would the factors mentioned below affect your choice of primary school?
Please try not to think only of the particular school you have chosen for your children, but your opinions generally.
Give your opinion by ticking the most appropriate box.

	Very important	Fairly important	Not really important	Completely unimportant	No view
a) The school's reputation					
b) Whether the school is often reported in the local press					
c) What you think of the Head					
d) What you think of the teachers					
e) The importance the school seems to place on parents' and pupils' views					
f) What you have heard the people in the neighbourhood say about the school					
g) What you know about the school from your own experience					
h) What you have seen of the behaviour of the pupils					
i) Other factors. Please write your ideas here and grade their importance.					

Question 2: How did the factors mentioned below affect your decis
about the particular primary school you chose?
Give your opinion by ticking the most appropriate box.

	Very important	Fairly important	Not really important	Completely unimportant	No view
a) The school's reputation					
b) Whether the school is often reported in the local press					
c) What you think of the Head					
d) What you think of the teachers					
e) The importance the school seems to place on parents' and pupils' views					
f) What you have heard the people in the neighbourhood say about the school					
g) What you know about the school from your own experience					
h) What you have seen of the behaviour of the pupils					
i) Other factors. Please write your ideas here and grade their importance.					

Question 3: Below is a list of factors which may affect the way any school is seen.
Give your opinion of their importance by ticking the most appropriate box.

	Very important	Fairly important	Not really important	Completely unimportant	No view
a) The number of 11+ passes/places gained at direct grant schools					
b) Litter around the school					
c) The care of the pupils shown by the school					
d) The state of repair of the exterior of the school buildings, fences, playgrounds, etc.					
e) The quality of presentation of the school's brochures, letters, etc.					
f) Pupil behaviour on entering /leaving the school					
g) School uniform policy					
h) Pupils' behaviour in the neighbourhood					
i) Content of school rules					
j) Access to the school's car park					
k) How well the school is equipped					

	Very important	Fairly important	Not really important	Completely unimportant	No view
l) Car parking facilities for parents					
m) The cleanliness of the classrooms and corridors					
n) Good press reports					
o) Bad press reports					
p) How visitors are treated					
q) The informal community grapevine					
r) The size of classes					
s) The nearness of the school					
t) The usefulness of the information provided, e.g. through visits, school brochures, etc.					
u) Discipline					
v) Quality of pupils' work on display					
w) Other factors. Please write your ideas below and grade their importance.					

Question 4: From Question 3, please pick out the five points you consider to be the most important and put them in order below.

1

2

3

4

5

Any additional comments

Question 5: You may have noticed that some primary schools set out to create a distinct school identity. The following factors are sometimes associated with this policy.
Please give your opinion of their effectiveness by ticking the most appropriate box.

	Very important	Fairly important	Not really important	Completely unimportant	No view
a) School uniform with definite style and colours					
b) School logo/crest on uniform and all documents					
c) School-wide codes of practice in the way all staff deal with parents, pupils and outside bodies					
d) School-wide policies on homework, reports, discipline, etc.					

Question 6:   Do you think that a primary school should try to have a definite identity of its own?

YES ☐   NO ☐   It doesn't matter ☐   Identity doesn't affect ☐
the image a school has

Question 7:   In what ways can a primary school improve its service to:

a) parents?

b) pupils?

c) the community?

Question 8:   Did you seek information about other primary schools in your area before making your choice? If so how?

Question 9:   Did you receive information about other primary schools in your area? If so what?

Question 10: What would you have liked more information about at that time?

Question 11: Here are some ways primary schools have tried to present a good image to the public in general and prospective parents in particular. How important do you feel it is, for a school to engage in such activities?

	Very important	Fairly important	Not really important	Completely unimportant	No view
a) Press/radio reports					
b) Inviting the public in					
c) Putting on musical/ dramatic productions for parents, etc.					

Question 12: Are the activities mentioned in Question 11 more important or less important than the school simply sticking to the basics of educating the pupils?

Question 13: Now that your child has started at this school, are there still things you feel you need to be told about, yet do not know? If so, what are they?

Question 14: What sort of a reputation has this school got in the community? Does it deserve such an image? On what is this reputation founded?

References

Beare, H., Caldwell, B.H., Millikan, R.H., *Creating an Excellent School*, Routledge Education, London, 1989.

Belbin, R. M., *Management Teams: Why they Succeed or Fail*, Heinemann, London, 1981.

Bell, L., *Management Skills in Primary Schools*, Routledge, London 1988.

Board of Education, *The McNair report* (para 168), 1944.

Bowles, G., Marketing and Promotion, in Fidler, B. and Bowles, G.(Eds), *Effective Local Management of Schools* (BEMAS), Longman, Essex, 1989.

Brunt, M., Marketing Schools in Craig, I. (Ed), *Primary School Management in Action*, Longman, Essex, 1987.

Coulson, A.A. and Cox, M., What Do Deputies Do? *Education 3 – 13,3,2*, 1975.

Day, C., Johnston, D. and Whitaker, P., *Managing Primary Schools*, Harper and Row, London, 1985.

Dean, J., *Managing the Primary School*, Croom Helm, Kent, 1987.

DES, *Children and their Primary Schools* (The Plowden Report), HMSO, London, 1967.

DES, *Primary Education in England*, HMSO, London, 1978.

DES, *Teachers' Pay and Conditions of Service*, HMSO, London (para. 32), 1988.

DES, *More Open Enrolment*, HMSO, London, 1989.

DES *School Teacher Appraisal: a National Framework* – Report of the National Steering Group on the School Teacher Appraisal, pilot study, HMSO, London, 1989.

DES, *Planning for School Development: Advice to Governors, Leaders and Teachers*, HMSO, London, 1989.

DES, *The Management and Development of Planning*, HMSO, London, 1990.

DES, *The Parents' Charter – you and your child's eduction*, HMSO, London, 1991.

DES, *Developing School Management* – report by the School
  Management Task Force, HMSO, London, 1991.
Devlin, T. and Knight, B., *Public Relations and Marketing for Schools*,
  Longman, London, 1981.
Dye, T.R., *Understanding Public Policy*, Englewood Cliffs, Prentice
  Hall, New Jersey, 1978.
Gittins, C., A Bursar in the Secondary School in Fidler, B. and Bowls,
  G., *Effective Local Management of Schools*, Longman, Essex, 1989.
Gorman, G., *Fund Raising for Schools*, Kogan Page, London, 1988.
Holly, P., and Southworth, G., *The Developing School*, Falmer,
  London, 1989.
ILEA, *Improving Primary Schools* (The Thomas Report), ILEA, 1985.
Joseph, K., *North of England Education Conference*, 6th January 1984,
  Sheffield, 1984.
Knight, B., *Managing School Time*, Longman, Essex, 1990.
Kotler, P. and Fox, K., *Strategic Marketing for Educational Institutions*,
  Prentice Hall, New York, 1985.
Lewin, K., The dynamics of group action, *Educational, Leadership, 1,
  195-200*, 1944.
Lockett, J., *Be the most effective Manager in your Business*, Thornsons,
  1987.
Macbeth, A., *Involving Parents*, Heinemann, London, 1989.
Marland, M., Rogers, R., *Marketing the School*, Heinemann, London,
  1991.
McMahon, A., Bolam, R. , Abbot, R. and Holly, P., *Guidelines for
  Review and Lateral Development in Schools*, Primary School
  Handbook, Longman/School Council, 1984.
Morgan, C. , Hall, V ., Mackay, H., *The Selection of Secondary
  Headteachers*, (The POST report), Open University Press, 1983.
Mortimore, P., Sammons, P., Stoll, L., Lewis, D., and Ecob, R., *The
  Junior School Project*, ILEA, London, 1986.
Mortimore, P. , Sammons, P., Stoll, L., Lewis, D., and
  Ecob, R., *School Matters*, Open Books, Froome, 1988.
Nash, I., Image-makers of the Sixth, *Times Educational Supplement*
  5.5.89, 1989.
Nias, J., Leadership Styles and Job Satisfaction in Primary Schools.
  In Bush, T., Glatter, R., Goodey, J. and Riches, C., (Eds),
  Approaches to School Management, Harper and Row, London, 1980.
Paisley, A. and Paisley A., *Effective Management in Primary Schools*,
  Basil Blackwell, Oxford, 1989.
Razzel, A., *Speech at North West Primary Adviser's Conference*,
  Manchester, 2.5.91, 1991.

Russell, A., *Promoting a Positive Image*, The Industrial Society, London, 1988.

Spooner, B., *Grey Eminence*, Gerbil, Books, Leeds, 1989.

Thompson, C., 'Monitoring Client Satisfaction in Schools – a marketing activity', *School Organisation*, Vol.9, No.2, 1989.

Tulloch, N. *School Choice and Appeal*, Ace, London, 1991.

West, M. and Bollington, R., *Teacher Appraisal*, David Fulton Ltd, London, 1990.

Whitaker, P., *The Primary Head*, Heinemann, London, 1983.

Winkley, D., A view from a primary school in Brighouse, T. and Moon, B. (Eds), *Managing the National Curriculum : some critical perspectives* (BEMAS), Longman, Essex, 1990.

Index